Towards Independent Reading

M. H. NEVILLE
and
A. K. PUGH

HEINEMANN EDUCATIONAL BOOKS
LONDON

Heinemann Educational Books Ltd
22 Bedford Square, London WC1B 3HH

LONDON   EDINBURGH   MELBOURNE   AUCKLAND
HONG KONG   SINGAPORE   KUALA LUMPUR   NEW DELHI
IBADAN   NAIROBI   JOHANNESBURG
EXETER (NH)   KINGSTON   PORT OF SPAIN

ISBN 0 435 10722 4

Printed and bound in Great Britain by Biddles Ltd of Guildford
and King's Lynn.
Photoset by GMGraphics, Harrow-on-the-Hill, Middlesex.

Contents

List of Tables

List of Figures

Preface

This book brings together a series of studies of reading in the 9–11 range which we have carried out over several years. It also reports on a more comprehensive study of twenty better and twenty poorer readers in their first year in a middle school. The report, in the third chapter of the book, is fairly self-contained and so may be read on its own: however, the earlier chapters give the background, both theoretical and practical (Chapter 1) and in terms of our earlier studies (Chapter 2), while the final chapter discusses implications of the research and offers suggestions and recommendations.

Research of the type we report needs the cooperation of schools and we are grateful to the many teachers (and children) who have made the studies possible. Particular thanks are due to Mr Harry Wanless, Headmaster of the Hugh Gaitskell Middle School, Leeds, and to his staff, especially Mrs Anna Watson. They have shown enthusiasm for our work and given encouragement and advice when tolerance of our disruptions was the most we could reasonably expect.

Thanks are also due to Mr Brian Page, Central Language Laboratories, The University of Leeds, for use of some of its equipment and to Mr Jack Tempest for help with recording and other technical matters. The Student Computing Service of the Open University gave considerable assistance in data analysis. Much of the marking and coding was done by Mary Pugh, who also helped in preparing the manuscript.

Mr Greg Brooks and Mr Harry Wanless kindly commented on parts of the manuscript which was skilfully typed by Miss Maureen Fox, Mrs Margaret Greaves and Mrs Victoria Senn.

The studies have been supported by small grants from The University of Leeds and the Open University. For these we are grateful.

Mary H Neville
A K Pugh

1

Reading in the Middle School: Theoretical and Practical Issues

INTRODUCTION

Although there is a debate about the purposes of education, there is little question that fluency and independence in reading are important effects of schooling. Their importance is emphasized by the frequent expressions of dissatisfaction with the standards in reading attained by school leavers, and the spectre of widespread adult illiteracy even in developed countries has caused concern.

The evidence of low standards and illiteracy is not to be accepted uncritically – indeed we shall criticize it in some respects – but concern is nevertheless warranted. In part this is because the notion of functional literacy leads to (apparently) ever rising standards to be attained; more seriously, in our view, it is because the weaknesses we identify in the evidence for poor reading standards, that is mainly the tests used, themselves betray a limited conception of what reading involves and what it is for.

This book is principally concerned with the teaching, rather than the testing, of reading. Nevertheless, the issue of testing is of some relevance since testing has an effect on what is taught . This need not necessarily be the direct 'backwash effect' of which there is now greater awareness in the literature on testing and examining (e.g. Gorman 1979, on the UK; Maas-de Brouwer and Samson Sluiter 1978, on foreign language reading testing in Holland). In the case of reading, which is not an established school subject at middle and secondary school level (cf. Pugh 1980), a major problem is in identifying what is to be taught. The standardized tests have largely served both to obscure what should be taught and to fail to provide useful criteria for evaluation.

Our prime concern, then, is with the teaching of reading at middle school level. This involves not only a consideration of methods but also, as we have stressed, an identification of what is to be taught. This identification, in turn, is not a simple matter which can be determined solely by reference to factors such as 'the needs of the child' – though his present capabilities and his current and future needs have to be taken into account. Nor can it be considered without reference to the environment in which the teaching occurs; at its simplest we have, for example, to recognize that teaching occurs in schools which are, in various ways, constrained. These constraints include, for example, finance, for lack of books hardly helps in developing reading (Educational Publishers' Association 1980); and staffing, for the quality of the head and the staff has considerable bearing on reading standards, more, in fact, than any other factor according to exhaustive studies by Morris (1966, p.297).

We make no apology for introducing what are often designated 'theoretical' concerns in this discussion. There are grounds for thinking that important changes take place in the style of reading of which children are capable – or at least which they normally adopt – around the top primary or lower middle-school level. They move from a model of reading which is (implicitly) based on oral reading to one which is closer to that employed by proficient adult silent readers. How they move between these stages has not been very fully investigated, although some knowledge of what is occurring (or at least what might be occurring) seems to us a necessary prerequisite for selecting appropriate teaching methods.

In Chapter 2 we report on a series of studies conducted over several years which have been addressed to questions of theoretical and practical importance for the teaching of reading to children in middle schools (hence also, upper primary and lower secondary levels). These studies, while we should not describe them as 'action research', were carried out mainly in one school and in very close cooperation with the staff so that methods we tried out and findings we passed on had an effect on subsequent teaching and, thus, on our

2

subsequent studies. After we had carried out these separate but related studies on matters such as reading while listening as a teaching method, change in style of reading discerned in cloze error analysis, and the use of books to locate information, it seemed sensible to apply the methods we had developed and the hypotheses we had formed to the study of one group of children. Thus some of the studies we report are with separate samples of children. In Chapter 3, we report a study 'in the round' of various aspects of the reading of a group of 40 children, half poorer readers and half better readers, in this transitional stage from oral to silent reading. Finally, we discuss some implications for practice and make some recommendations.

In this present chapter we provide a more detailed discussion of issues we have already raised relating to theoretical, methodological and practical concerns in the teaching of reading at lower middle-school level.

THEORETICAL FRAMEWORK

There are numerous models of reading development and of the reading process. A useful collection is given by Singer and Ruddell (1976). However, few models are adequate for practical application (Geyer 1972), and a good many are, in fact, based one on another, their genealogies being of some interest in their own right but revealing a lack of attention to the phenomenon of reading itself (cf. Brooks 1980a). Psychological models of reading which take no account of the normal reading situation have been criticized (e.g. Pugh 1978 and Stubbs 1980 who argues for a sociolinguistic perspective on reading and literacy). Also, so-called developmental models which do not much concern themselves with reading processes seem unlikely to be of much help. However, process models of, for example, reading in adults may well be worthwhile since developmental models can be built from them, as we shall show.

A good deal of the argument in the educational literature about the reading process (usefully reviewed in, for example, Downing 1979) has centred on whether one should adopt a model of reading which involves 'mere decoding' or one which recognizes some more complex information-processing activity. In many respects this may not seem to be a very fruitful argument because reading, especially in schools, is a construct rather than a natural phenomenon. In other words, what 'reading' is taken to involve might be word recognition, cloze completion, rapid reading of text or whatever else it is decided shall be called reading for particular children in a particular class. The view that the argument over models is, in fact, over what should be taught is relevant since it relates to our emphasis on the importance of deciding what to teach (rather than how to teach it). The practical importance of the decision may be seen in early reading schemes. If one adopts the view that reading involves discrimination between minimal pairs, as did the linguist Bloomfield (cf. Bloomfield and Barnhart 1961), then decoding exercises which also teach rules of 'the cat sat on the mat' variety are likely to ensue. If, on the other hand, a different emphasis in linguistics is adopted then the importance of children recognizing the communicative function of reading will be stressed (as in *Breakthrough to Literacy*, Mackay *et al*. 1970).

Now, while we incline to the functional, communicative view, it must be recognized that reading aloud has been widely used as a means of beginning reading both in developed countries and in the Third World, as it was in Victorian England; and indeed attempts to start children reading silently as in McDade's experiment (Buswell 1945: see Pugh 1978, p.19) have not been very successful or widespread. As Conrad (1972) suggests, there are several possible explanations for the almost universal adoption of reading aloud as a means for beginning reading; nevertheless the reading-aloud-to-teacher approach is justly not without its critics, especially as it requires a rapid switch for many children entering school in their perception of what reading involves which could usefully be mitigated (see for example Cashdan 1980, Reid 1972).

The model which a school adopts is, therefore, important for the learners. In considering the model, however, more attention needs to be paid to the goal of the teaching, i.e. the proficient adult reader, so that there is some clear idea of the direction the teaching should take. The considerable psychological literature on adult reading has recently focussed on the processing of information and particularly on modelling of memory in terms of computer function. For example, Atkinson and Shiffrin (1968) posited the existence of a sensory register (for selection of perceptions), short-term store (as a working memory) and a long-term store. Baddeley (1976) gives a useful review of studies in memory and Seymour (1979) provides a thorough discussion of recent work in this field, with some particular reference to reading. He deals especially with the problem of how information received in one form (e.g. graphemic in reading) can be nevertheless used in other forms, and what the implications of this are for storage in (long-term) memory. Work in this area has been influenced by the positing of the existence of a logogen system, which permits recognition, production and silent thinking about each word we use (see Morton 1979).

The ramifications of this research are considerable but we may stress that, in general, the studies have been of words in isolation or in small groups rather than of text and we should point out that the existence of words as discrete units in modes other than writing is in some doubt. Thus the relevance to early reading may not be so strong and greater emphasis should perhaps be given to the reader/text interaction, an area which only recently has received much attention (e.g. Otto *et al*. 1980, Pugh 1981a).

Nevertheless, models based on this work in memory are of importance for stressing the information-processing aspect of reading and, hence, the adoption of 'psycholinguistic' models of reading in schools. Smith (1971, 1973) has perhaps been most influential in making known this emphasis on information processing but the developmental model which we have found useful is due to Goodman (1968), another important writer on the psycholinguistics of reading.

Goodman suggests three levels or stages of reading proficiency, which we have designated the oral, the aural and the silent stages. He also allows for adult reading aloud, but sees this as a rather different activity from the oral reading of children. At the oral stage the child has to recode graphic input (letters, letter patterns and word shapes) into phonemic patterns, which provide an aural input which the child recodes into speech before, finally, decoding to obtain meaning. At the aural stage larger graphic sequences can be dealt with and these can be simultaneously matched with aural input for

5

recoding into oral language (if necessary) to obtain meaning. Finally, at the silent stage, the various operations are collapsed so that meaning is obtained directly from the text.

While we have found the developmental aspects of the model useful, we should nevertheless query the assumption in it that adult readers can go directly to the meaning of a text. The answer to the question of how we arrive at meaning to some extent seems to depend on the psychological tradition in which researchers are working. Thus Goodman is following the American tradition (exemplified in, for example, Gibson and Levin, 1975, but with much deeper roots) that a purely visual reading is possible; another tradition, more common in Russia, emphasizes the mediation of oral language in all reading. The experimental evidence appears to support the Russian view (e.g. Edfeldt 1959, Sokolov 1968; and cf. the review in Conrad 1972), while the difficulties encountered by the deaf in learning to read suggest that, at least at earlier stages, some kind of inner speech is helpful in reading (Conrad 1979, Kyle 1980).

The earlier stages are less contentious than this third stage. Although again relatively little is known about the processing which takes place, Goodman's model would probably gain fairly wide support as an indication of the way reading development takes place in education. This leaves aside the question whether it *need* take place in this way, though we have already noted that this is the pattern of learning to read in many cultures. It may, therefore, have a firm basis.

The implications of the second stage have not been thoroughly examined, and it is part of the purpose of this book to consider them further. If the child is using both graphic and aural input, then features such as the intonation pattern of the author (as reconstituted by the reader) are aiding his under-standing. On the other hand, his use of a text is hindered by the constraint placed on him by having to read in a fairly even paced and sequential manner in order to take advantage of what the text would sound like if read aloud.

It is surprising that intonation in reading has received little attention, for the development of familiarity with intonation patterns, which in many respects are unlike those of normal (conversational) speech, is an important aspect of reading development at this level. On the other hand, dependence on

6

them has to disappear if the reader is to be able to take full advantage of the freedom which proficiency in silent reading brings in dealing with texts. For example, a silent reader can skim through material rapidly, without processing it in detail, in order to locate the part he wants to read.

It may be that this withering away of dependence on oral features of processing itself mirrors the gradual move from reading aloud word by word, via reading *sotto voce* with minimal lip movement, to the aural stage we are now concerned with. However, Goodman's model tells us little about this nor does it explain the recourse to varying degrees of inner speech in adult reading, notably an increase in its incidence as text becomes more difficult. In fairness to Goodman it must be noted that he stresses that the stages are not discrete even if he does not point to the limits. Other writers with an information-processing perspective (e.g. Laberge and Samuels 1974) have argued that automatization of skill in lower-level reading tasks is what permits development from stage to stage. In discussions of models of this kind there is often a suggestion that adult process models can both take account of the type of development we have suggested *and* allow for recourse, by adults faced with difficulties or reading for specialized purposes, to types of reading normally found at earlier stages.

Not all models are concerned with the role of inner speech. Ulijn has employed the following model for understanding text by adults which shows the interaction of text, lexicon (i.e. store of 'words') and conceptual system and indicates two-way eye to brain feedback.

Figure 1 The reader in man (Ulijn 1980, p.27)

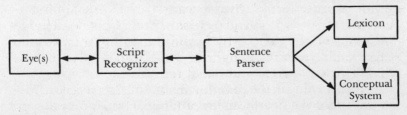

This model relates to another old but important question as to what drives what in reading, whether the brain dictates what the eyes see or vice versa. The issue is resolved in this model by suggesting both, and the question of conversion from one medium to another is not dealt with. There appear to be three main views on this central question: *direct* processing, as in Goodman's third level, where understanding in adults stems from visual input and any phonological coding is *post hoc*, and unessential for understanding; *mediated* processing, like Goodman's second stage, where visual input is mediated by 'translation' into a phonological form; and *parallel* processing, which might involve an 'articulatory loop', a refinement proposed by several writers and shown in a model from Brooks (1980b). In Brooks's model (see Fig. 2) the reader chooses (though this is normally done without a conscious decision) whether to use articulatory or phonological processing; in our terms, whether to revert to aural and/or oral stages.

Figure 2 Model of the reading process (Brooks 1980b)

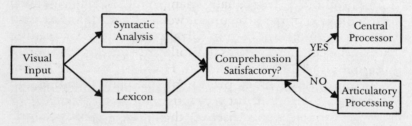

This model appears somewhat like Ulijn's 'Reader in Man' (see Fig. 1) but it shows rather more clearly what directs the processing, i.e. the comprehension check makes the reader decide whether he can understand from visual input or whether he needs recourse to aural or oral help. Such a model has an advantage over Goodman's in that it suggests how the stages can be interrelated.

This discussion of models may seem to have taken us some way from reading in the middle school. In fact it has not, for as we have argued a clearer understanding of both processes and development in reading is necessary if appropriate teaching and testing are to be undertaken. Hence, we have attempted in studies described later in the book to examine which types or stages of reading are employed by the middle school age-group. In particular, it is because this age-group appears, following the models, to be a transitional one, that its study is both theoretically interesting and of strong practical concern. Since different readers may well require quite different teaching, the practical implications are considerable.

METHODS OF TESTING AND STUDY

Oral reading apart, reading behaviour is very difficult to test and to study. Not only is the process inaccessible, most of it taking place in the 'black box' of the brain, but the output of reading is also difficult to capture, since what is achieved from (real life) reading with comprehension is often a modification of the conceptual system, not just the addition of bits of information. An explanation of what is meant here may be given by analogy with importing a new word into the language. The adoption in Middle English of the term 'marriage' was not a simple addition. It gradually changed the use of terms such as wedding, restricted the use of wedlock and did away with 'Marry!' as used as an oath in Elizabethan times. So, reading with understanding changes in subtle ways the organization of information in the reader's mind. However, since we do not know how it is organized prior to any particular reading and have no way of finding out very satisfactorily, either before or after, we cannot readily discover the effect of reading. Some research has been addressed to problems of this kind in the past few years, particularly in studies of the structure of recalled information related to the structure of text (see, for example, Marshall and Glock 1978, Tierney and Mosenthal 1980).

These studies, though promising and important, do not immediately concern us here, except that they indicate how problematical the subject is. In particular, recent research in cognitive psychology has confirmed the naivety of many studies and measures of comprehension. This has, of course, been recognized for some time and acknowledged by earlier researchers (see, for example, Farr 1969, Lunzer, Waite and Dolan 1979). Indeed, one of us (Pugh 1978) in giving a fuller review of the topic of comprehension has argued that the term itself is a misnomer and that 'apprehension' might be more appropriate.

Other studies, again reviewed in more detail elsewhere (Pugh 1978, Levy-Schoen and O'Regan 1979) have concentrated on visual behaviour during reading and paid relatively little attention to comprehension. However, there are many technical problems which exacerbate difficulties of research design, especially in that they preclude reading under relatively normal conditions. Apart from this direct observation of reading and the study of comprehension using reports of what has been read, or answers to questions on the reading, several other approaches have been used in studying reading. These include the eye-voice span (see Levin 1979) in which a measure is taken of the time interval in reading aloud between the position of the eye and the audible sound; tachistoscopic experiments in which the (usually short) text is exposed for a very limited duration; cloze procedure in which words are deleted from a text and the subject must supply these missing words; and other variants of this approach with reduplicated words, scrambled text and so on (Heaton 1975 gives a useful guide to approaches of this kind).

Now, it is not only the problems of studying reading which have bearing on testing, but the research methods themselves seem to have had some effect on the types of test used. At the level we are concerned with, there are very few tests specifically designed for either diagnostic or evaluative purposes. Buros (1978) in his standard American reference work lists relatively few tests for the middle school level, while Pumfrey (1976) in a useful survey of tests used in the United Kingdom shows that there are very few British tests indeed for the age-group we are concerned with. In the main it seems that word recognition tests, where the child reads a word aloud, are commonly used; there is a series of graded test passages followed by comprehension questions (Neale 1966); there are sentence completion tests (e.g. *NFER Test AD,* Watts 1970); and there are two cloze tests, the GAP (McLeod and Unwin 1970) and the GADAPOL (McLeod and Anderson 1973). None of these is a diagnostic test and there must be reservations about what they actually test. Sentence completion tests, widely used in survey testing, may be drawing heavily on verbal reasoning, though they have been defended by Start and Wells (1972) who argue that they were suitable for use in NFER national surveys since they measured 'whether one could read in some measure like an educated man' (pp. 16-17). Nevertheless, they have been replaced as a result of work at the NFER on behalf of the Assessment of Performance Unit of the DES; the new tests are based on several passages which are to be read for different purposes. This approach is an extension, in that a wider range of texts and purposes are included, of that used in the *Edinburgh Reading Tests* . There are four batteries: stage two, which includes tests intended for the younger end of the age-range we are concerned with, has separate scores for six aspects of reading (Godfrey Thomson Unit 1980).

Of the other types of test, word recognition tests are not valid measures of what occurs in reading at the level we are concerned with, being more appropriate to the earlier oral stage. This does not mean that they necessarily lack predictive validity, i.e. they may measure something closely akin to, or more likely prerequisite for, fluent reading. Cloze tests and the Neale test have been used (as have sentence completion tests) in the studies reported later in the book. Some of their limitations will become apparent, both as measures of achievement and, particularly, because they give little diagnostic information of relevance to our concerns.

As regards studying reading, we have used tests as indicated, together with observation of visual and motor behaviour when using a book and, where appropriate, interview and question-naire. These methods are also presented more fully later. We may mention at this point, however, that the variety of tests, taken with the paucity of them, suggests some uncertainty over what constitutes reading at this level.

We may also note that the difficulties over observing and assessing reading behaviour must cast doubt on figures given for adult illiteracy. These are, in fact, usually based on extrapolations from the results of sentence completion tests given at school, with the assumption that the results are sound and that no improvement has taken place after leaving. Rather rarely are they based on standardized tests given to adults, and the data available are very mixed (see Jones and Charnley 1978).

Reading is not normally treated as a school subject beyond the oral reading stage. After the infant school it tends to merge with English until it becomes lost in it. We have argued that reading is difficult to isolate in any case, and the fact that it is an essential skill for studying many subjects, but receives prime attention in none, adds to the problems.

According to a recent survey by Her Majesty's Inspectors of Schools (DES 1978, pp.45 and 47) there is, in their view, indeed a problem in primary schools. Although they noted a rise in standards (on sentence completion tests) between 1955 and 1976-7, they were concerned about lack of opportunity to extend pupils' range of reading. The 'basic techniques' of reading were well taught but at age eleven, pupils were too often being given graded readers so that 'advanced reading skills' were not being taught, few children discussed books at more than a superficial level of comprehension, and not enough could use books with ease and confidence as a source of information.

The aims implied here are of 'profit and delight', of both reading for information and for pleasure, and the suggestion of the Inspectors is that following set schemes of books, often with comprehension exercises, hinders the development of both. A more systematic approach is needed, they argue, and they concur with the recommendation in the Bullock Report (DES 1975) that every school should have a teacher with special responsibility for language and reading.

This does not mean that they consider that reading should become a 'subject' but it is a recognition that it requires special consideration. At secondary level, the Bullock Report rejected the idea of introducing the practice, common in some parts of the United States, of having reading as a subject (DES 1975, pp.116-17). Thus in secondary schools it is likely to form part of English, though English already has a range of almost contradictory trends which threaten its unity and coherence, and has not been noted for its concern with skills such as reading (Pugh 1980, 1981b).

We have not, so far, mentioned middle schools in this section though it is that age-range which interests us. In fact, the age-range is less clear than we have implied since the age of children in middle schools varies in different Education Authorities and indeed some authorities have no such schools. Related to this diversity in what constitutes middle schools, is lack of any clear agreement on how their curriculum should be organized. This stems in part from the recency of middle schools and from their position between the child-centred curriculum of the primary school and the subject-based one of secondary education. The curriculum of middle schools has been much discussed. For example, the results of the Schools Council *Middle Years of Schooling* Project (Badcock *et al.* 1972, Ross *et al.* 1975) give full discussion of aims and objectives and provide some suggested syllabuses. However, a great deal of flexibility remains in interpretations of what middle schools should do.

What is clear is that middle schools are less rigidly subject-orientated than secondary schools, yet have considerably more subjects and more specialist teachers than do primary schools. As there are no external examinations the curriculum is very much less constrained than that of the secondary school although external examinations do exert some indirect influence, especially for older children. In general, though, there is a great deal of opportunity for trying out different approaches at middle school level, including perhaps paying more systematic attention to reading.

In fact, a number of approaches to developing reading at this level have been suggested and employed, though possibly not in a systematic way. Cloze procedure has become quite widely used, partly because of an emphasis on it in influential Open University courses, possibly also because, as Merritt (1970) has argued, it appears to involve the kind of reading necessary at what he calls the intermediate stages. (We have reservations as to whether this is actually so, as explained in Chapter 2.) Reading laboratories have been popular for some time; reading while listening has also been used, especially perhaps because of the ready availability of BBC materials. These materials are not principally intended for this age-range, however. For lower secondary level Dolan *et al.* (1979) have advocated and examined group activities, including several based on sequencing and prediction (e.g. of story ending) and Walker (1974) has also proposed activities of a similar nature. Others have stressed the importance of teaching

13

the uses of reading, whether in terms of the 'sociolinguistics' of reading (Stubbs 1980) or simply by clarifying the range of styles of reading available to the proficient adult reader (Pugh 1978). Wide availability of reading materials has often been held to be important with some writers suggesting that exposure to books and immersion in them is what is needed. This view currently under investigation in primary schools in the Bradford Book Flood Experiment (see Ingham 1980). Use of books for information has also been stressed both indirectly, by the use of project work, and more directly in numerous books on library use and study skills. It must, regrettably, be said that many of these (e.g. Herring 1978) concentrate unduly on such matters as the Dewey system and stress the organization of the library; the advice on how to use books is rather bland and too generalized, often based on assumptions which are not well-founded.

This is a problem which we also address in later chapters, for 'skills' of this kind can probably not be well taught without reference to subject matter. A need for help with them still seems to exist, even at sixth-form level, however (Dean *et al.* 1979), and among university students (Pugh 1978).

These methods of developing reading we have mentioned provide in general little more than a context for reading, often with some motivation as in the 'guessing' aspect of cloze and group sequencing. Reading while listening, however, seems to us both to mirror the kind of reading done at the aural stage and to be likely to assist it. By providing the intonation patterns for the reader and reducing his mental load, it frees him to attend to (and even enjoy) aspects of reading other than decoding. However, as we have suggested there may be certain dangers in that it may inculcate a style of reading inappropriate for silent reading. We have, therefore, as we describe in more detail in the next chapters, been concerned both with reading while listening and with the use of books for information. In addition, we have used cloze procedure, though as a testing device and a research tool, rather than as a teaching method. Nevertheless, we note some implications for the use of cloze in teaching.

Discussion of method alone is not enough: as we have already stressed, the aims of teaching reading at middle school level also need careful examination. The Bullock Report (DES

14

1975) suggested the following as major emphases in the middle years: consolidation of the work of earlier years, with special help where necessary; 'to maintain and extend the idea of reading as an activity which brings great pleasure and is a personal resource of limitless value'; 'to develop the pupils' reading from the general to the more specialized, (p.115). The drift may be uncontentious, though it is hard to see what exactly is meant by general to more specialized, and greater specificity than this will be needed if one is to discern 'a clear line of development' which the Bullock Report considered teachers should recognize throughout reading education. This is not, of course, to deny the importance of fuller understanding of these patterns of development.

CONCLUSION

In fact, there has been little attention paid to theoretical issues or to practical methods and curriculum concerns with regard to reading at middle school level. The Bullock Report has little to say about the middle years; its chapter titles move from the Early Stages to the Later Stages without pausing long in between. There are problems related not only to method and to lack of theoretical bases. Middle schools are not generally established, and where they do exist they cater for different age-ranges in different geographical areas. They are likely to lean towards either the primary school or the secondary school in finding a model for their curriculum.

Conversely, the fluidity of organization of education and of curriculum at this level provides an opportunity for giving particular attention to reading. In the view of the Bullock Report and of the H. M. Inspectors' Report, such attention is needed. We offer here both empirical evidence about methods, and studies which cast light on theoretical issues. This will, we hope, provide a contribution to more specific and productive examination and discussion of reading in the middle school.

2

The Middle Stages:
Studies of Reading Styles and Abilities

INTRODUCTION

Over several years we have conducted a series of distinct but related studies of aspects of reading in children aged about ten, that is the first year of middle school in many education authorities. These studies are grouped for the purposes of this chapter as follows: investigations of styles of reading using cloze procedure; reading while listening as a teaching method; use of books for location of information. Some other relevant research which we have carried out is also referred to, mainly that relating to older children. We do not attempt here a full review of the literature on relevant topics such as cloze procedure; our purpose is to give brief descriptions of the methods and main findings of our studies, as these may be useful in themselves and are necessary background for the larger, more comprehensive study reported in Chapter 3, which deals with these and other aspects of reading at the middle school level.

STUDIES OF READING STYLES USING CLOZE PROCEDURE

Cloze procedure is a technique in which words in a text are deleted, usually at regular intervals (typically every fifth, seventh, or tenth word) and the deleted text is then given to subjects for completion. Often a 'run in' passage of undeleted text precedes the section containing the gaps. Cloze procedure has been fairly widely used in teaching, assessment and research since it was advocated by Taylor (1953) as a means of assessing the readability of newspapers. Its use as a teaching technique owes much to 'psycholinguistic' emphases in the 1960s which stemmed from information theory (notably Shannon 1948) and from the application of work of this kind (in Merritt, 1970) to reading. The Open University courses on reading development have, no doubt, done much to foster the use of cloze procedure in British schools, although its use in teaching is not unquestioned. (A useful recent annotated bibliography with contains reference to criticisms of its applications to teaching is KcKenna and Robinson 1980.)

A good deal of discussion of cloze procedure for testing has centred on what deletion rates should be used. This question is examined fully by Bormuth (1973) who also discussed the problem of how to interpret the scores achieved in cloze tests. The interpretation of cloze test scores when testing readability poses particular problems, even though cloze procedure seems more promising than readability formulae in that it actually involves reader and text in interaction.

It is an oddly mutilated text which the reader interacts with, however, and the extent to which cloze completion mirrors normal reading behaviour is questionable as Gibson (1972) remarked during the heyday of research using cloze procedure. Nevertheless, and despite some recent concern on matters such as the use of unstandardized passages and varying marking procedures (e.g. Alderson 1979, Douglas 1978), cloze procedure does form a useful means of examining errors made by readers in non-oral reading.

Error analysis, often called miscue analysis and most commonly applied to reading aloud, has also become well known through 'psycholinguistic' work in the 1960s. Goodman's *Taxonomy of Oral Reading Miscues* (Goodman 1969) has been used both as a diagnostic instrument for teachers and as a research tool (for example, recently by Thomson 1978, in comparing dyslexic and normal readers). Influential work by Weber (1970) and by Clay (1972) has also been directed towards oral reading errors. This line of work has also, of course, not been without its critics, for example Potter (1980) who considers modifications are needed to procedures used to avoid confounding graphic and linguistic factors.

The emphasis in work concerned with miscues on linguistic constraints provided the basis for our own studies. It seemed likely that examination of errors and omissions, by type as well as frequency in a cloze test, could cast some light on the strategies used by children. The method appeared to be suitable from a practical point of view for testing fairly large numbers and for multiple retesting. It seemed prudent to ensure that the passages used in retesting were comparable, and preferable to have texts known to be suitable for the age-range and for which standardization information was available. A standardized cloze test, the GAP test (McLeod and Unwin 1970), became available in Britain at about the time we started these studies. Two parallel forms (Red and Blue) were published and although the British standardization data were not very complete (the test was developed in Australia), it was preferable to use this test than to prepare our own passages and hence be drawn into test construction rather than studies of performance on cloze tasks.

In our first study (Neville and Pugh 1974) we compared performance in parallel forms of the GAP test given as reading tests and listening tests. The subjects were 66 children of normal reading ability, aged 8 years 10 months to 10 years 9 months. They were divided into two similar groups. One of the groups received a listening version of form R (the Red version) and the normal cloze reading version of form B (the Blue version); the other group received the reading version of form R and the listening version of form B. The listening tests were specially prepared so that a ten-second interval occurred at each gap. During this interval the subjects should write down (on an answer sheet) the missing word. We had scores also from a sentence completion test (NFER *Reading Test AD*, Watts 1970) for these subjects.

Since in the listening version, the subjects have only the preceding text to help them, whereas in reading all the text is available, analysis of errors could reveal differences between the modes; it might also show that some children used strategies in their reading more akin to those they used in listening and, hence, more appropriate to reading aloud than to silent reading. There were, it was recognized, problems in comparing reading while listening and it could not be predicted how far listening might relatively favour the poorer readers nor, indeed, how much harder or more difficult the listening test would be in comparison with the reading test. In the listening version, on the one hand there would be no problems over 'unknown words' and the intonation of the reader would help; on the other hand, the subjects had only the preceding context, a time limit of ten seconds to supply a word, they could not go back, and listening may present its own problems, especially in this type of task.

Correlational analyses showed that those who were better at reading (as judged by scores from the school's administration of sentence completion test AD) were also better at reading in the GAP test ($r = .80$, $p < .01$). They were significantly better at listening too, though the correlation coefficient was much lower ($r = .50$, $p < .01$). GAP reading and GAP listening were similarly correlated ($r = .48$, $p < .01$). Inspection of these coefficients suggests that GAP reading and listening are significantly but not very highly correlated.

Scores for the reading tests overall were significantly greater than for the listening test (mean 24.60, s.d. 5.22 for reading: mean 13.87, s.d. 5.53 for listening; $t = 5.93$, $p < .001$). The two groups were found to be similar as regards reading ability and hence with these children the equivalence of the means for the two forms of the test of reading was established. In the listening version, however, the groups differed significantly according to which listening test was taken (form B mean 17.81, s.d. 4.39; form R mean 10.18, s.d. 3.53; $t = 7.74$, $p < .001$). Reasons for this were clarified in examining the errors.

The error analysis was carried out as follows. Each gap was examined. Correct responses were ticked and then ignored. Omissions were counted, as were actual errors. The errors were categorized in terms of their appropriateness in relation to the correct word (as given in the test manual). Some words offered were wholly inappropriate. Others were wrong but of the same part of speech (*syntactically* appropriate), or had the same root (*semantically* appropriate). Those of the same part of speech could also be correct as regards tense, number and other morphological features (*syntactically* and *morphologically* appropriate), and those with the same root could be of the same part of speech (*semantically and syntactically* appropriate). An example is as follows. One of the items in form R of the

Table 1 Frequencies of type of error in Forms B and R of the GAP tests (percentages in parentheses)

Test and Form	Omissions	Wholly inappropriate	Incorrect but appropriate				Total
			Syntactically	Syntactically and morphologically	Semantically	Syntactically and semantically	
Reading R	21 (4)	270 (51)	34 (6)	169 (32)	–	34 (7)	528
Reading B	58 (9)	259 (43)	34 (6)	195 (32)	32 (5)	32 (5)	610
Listening R	186 (17)	514 (47)	72 (7)	280 (26)	–	31 (3)	1083
Listening B	204 (27)	249 (33)	43 (6)	214 (28)	20 (3)	22 (3)	752

GAP test is: She sang with the ____ as they chirped in the hedges. 'Birds' is the correct word according to the manual. 'Boys' would be wrong but would be appropriate syntactically (same part of speech) and morphologically (same number, i.e. plural). 'Bird' would be appropriate semantically and syntactically. The results of this kind of analysis are shown in Table 1.

Errors made in the two reading versions were similar in pattern ($x^2 = 1.99$, p $<$ .05), but there was a significant difference in pattern of errors between the two listening tests overall ($x^2 = 24.43$, p $<$ .001). Form B was similar with regard to type of error whether used for reading or listening ($x^2 = 6.64$, p $<$ .05) but form R differed ($x^2 = 9.63$, p $<$ .05). Inspection revealed fewer syntactically appropriate errors than expected in form R in the listening mode as compared to the reading mode and a higher frequency of other types of error. There were significantly more omissions in the listening mode in both forms (Red $x^2 = 57.31$, p $<$ .001; Blue $x^2 = 60.4$, p $<$ .001) and significantly more omissions in the Blue version in both modes than the Red version ($x^2 = 15.9$, p $<$ .001 for listening; $x^2 = 26.27$, p $<$ .001 for reading).

Form R of the test had more blanks near the beginning of sentences and this appeared likely to be the cause of difficulty resulting in the large number of omissions in both modes. However, there was no clear evidence that mode, whether reading or listening, affected the type of error made, though some weaknesses in the GAP test seemed to be revealed. For the comparison between styles of reading a design which included dichotomized groups of better and poorer readers seemed necessary.

A second study was, therefore, undertaken (Neville and Pugh 1976). For this study an additional version of the test was employed, in the form of a booklet which subjects had to work through sequentially and each page of which contained all the preceding context up to a gap. This was in an attempt to reduce any interference from factors other than contextual constraints which may have affected the reading/listening comparison in the previous study.

Subjects were 130 children aged between nine and ten years. These were children in the first year of middle school whereas those in the previous study were in their penultimate year of primary school.

Procedure was substantially similar to the previous study, except that there were four groups of children. It was found that scores for the restricted reading (i.e. in the booklet) were similar to those for listening and that scores for reading were significantly higher than for either of the other modes (t ranged from 2.08 to 3.02 for the four groups, p < .05 for one group and < .01 for the others). However, when the sample was divided into 'better' and 'poorer' readers a different picture emerged. For better readers there was a highly significant difference (p < .001) between score on reading and score in the other mode (i.e. listening or restricted reading), but for the poorer readers there was no significant difference.

The linguistic analysis of errors yielded results substantially similar to those in previous study, in that no clear overall pattern emerged of type of error in relation to mode of presentation. Nor did better or poorer readers differ significantly with regard to patterns of error when their responses were compared, as before, with the target words. Once again, however, there was evidence to question the equivalence of the two forms (Red and Blue) especially when used in modes other than silent reading. Also, it was found that more guesses were made in the restricted reading (booklet) than in listening, since although the scores were comparable there were fewer incompleted gaps in the booklet.

Since the analysis into types of error in relation to the target word did not yield significant differences, it was suspected that analysis in relation to context might do so. Because of large numbers of omissions on later items, responses to twelve of the earlier gaps were considered. These were gaps at the beginning or middle of sentences where the correct response depended on subsequent information – syntactic or semantic – in the same sentence. Twelve 'critical' gaps – seven in form R and five in form B – were studied. These all occurred before gap eighteen in either form since most of the subjects attempted to fill gaps up to this point (the median score was 19).

The results (Table 2) indicated that there was a highly significant difference ($\chi^2 = 11.76$, p < .001) between the two levels when errors in relation to context were compared for the reading versions. These differences were not found in restricted

Table 2 Frequencies of types of incorrect responses
in relation to context

Incorrect responses for 12 'gaps'	Upper reading level			Lower reading level		
	Reading	Booklet	Listening	Reading	Booklet	Listening
Suitable in total context	26*	7	7	38*	5	6
Suitable in context preceding 'gaps'	19*	70	66	92*	90	78
Unsuitable to either context above	0	3	0	18*	7	6
Total	45*	80	73	148*	102	90

*The N of subjects for reading test is twice that of subjects for booklet and listening tests

reading ($\chi^2 = .503$) nor in listening ($\chi^2 = .098$). Inspection of Table 2 reveals that the better readers gave proportionately more responses which, though incorrect, were suitable to total context and fewer which were suitable in the light of preceding context only.

From these studies, therefore, it seemed that the context is used differently (and differentially) by better and poorer readers, that judging responses against the target word rather than the context does not reveal these differences, but that they are revealed by comparisons of errors in cloze reading and restricted reading or listening when context is taken into account. From this it was decided in the broader investigation reported in Chapter 3 to pursue the question of use of context further and to ensure that groups used in the sample should clearly dichotomize better and poorer readers.

Some work not so far reported was also done in attempting to devise a simple diagnostic test which would differentiate readers who made use of full context (and might, therefore, be assumed to be using a style of reading similar to that of proficient adults) from those who relied heavily on preceding context. It had been noted that the sentence completion tests which, oral reading scales apart, are most commonly used at this age-level normally required completion at or near the end of a sentence. Various pilot studies were made in which cloze tests were prepared with what were judged to be strategically placed deletions. However, one appeal of cloze procedure is the apparent ease with which a test can be prepared (even though interpretation, validity and reliability of results are problematical). Therefore, passages were also prepared in which a simple procedure applicable to other texts was employed; after a run in, the first word of one sentence, the last word of the next, the first word of the fourth and so on, were deleted.

Further trials of this approach to diagnostic testing were made as part of the study in Chapter 3 and findings are reported there where theoretical, testing and teaching concerns are examined together.

READING WHILE LISTENING AS A TEACHING METHOD

Our studies of reading while listening were more obviously related to the practical concerns of teachers than were the studies just described, although they are also of theoretical interest. If we are right in positing an aural stage in the development of reading, then the use of aural input could well provide considerable assistance while reading for some children, and help others to reach the aural stage.

The idea of learning to read by listening to others reading while following in a text is not new. It was the normal method of learning to read in the nineteenth century, though often at the expense of understanding what was read. Where understanding was considered important, one teachers' manual advised, '*Do not permit too much to be read at one time*. A good teacher can profitably occupy twenty or thirty minutes over a page, without at all wearying his children' (Henry Dunn, cited Goldstrom 1972, p.150). Similar detailed *explication de texte* appears to have been suffered by Huey (1908) who writes of 'hours of listless poring over uninteresting texts' and, indeed, is still criticized in the French-speaking countries nowadays by Blampain (1979) who argues that school reading prevents the normal interaction of reader with text.

Reaction against such close reading and recognition of the need to develop fluency led to the silent reading movement in the United States (see Pugh 1978). The theories about the ill-effects of vocalizing in reading which this movement espoused found their way into the textbooks and tended to inhibit dependence on aural help with reading. Elsewhere, in Muslim countries for example, and in Ethiopia (see Ferguson 1971), hearing and memorizing of text for learning to read continued. Also, in the United States, linguists such as Fries (1963) and Lefevre (1964) tended to stress the importance of knowledge of the intonation patterns of what was read in developing reading fluency.

One of us (Neville 1968) was influenced by this and other work in psychology which stressed the role of speech in learning to read. A study was made to test the hypothesis that giving beginning readers an echoic or oral response before silent reading will, by encouraging the application of intonation patterns to reading, improve achievement and fluency and also reduce vocalization. Support was found for the hypothesis in the results, in that fluency improved and vocalization was reduced in groups that heard the oral reading and also when they read aloud themselves. However, in this experiment, reading accuracy and comprehension were not affected by mode of response. Thus we were extremely cautious in some early pilot studies with foreign students of low English proficiency who were attending a British university, that we should not cause them to revert to a style of reading which depended on vocalization, a style which much of the literature appeared to suggest would be very harmful. On the other hand the literature appeared to offer little for students whose knowledge of English was insufficient for them to develop fluency by guided practice in silent reading, except perhaps the reading aloud activities which these students had, in any case, elsewhere. Reading aloud in learning a foreign language may be important for various reasons, as argued by, for example, Beattie (1974), but it does not provide a model of fluent reading.

The BBC's *Listening and Reading* materials, introduced in the early 1970s were devised in reaction to the reading aloud of structured schemes by young readers and were intended to provide an experience of reading enjoyable material, which would normally be beyond the capacity of the reader if he were attempting the books solo. Also at this time there was considerable interest in rate-altered speech, whereby tape recordings can be mechanically or electronically changed in rerecording so that the message appears faster or slower. This technique, covered in a comprehensive three-volume bibliography (Duker 1974), seemed suitable for overcoming a problem mentioned by the BBC in the notes on *Listening and Reading* that some children, especially initially, found the recordings too fast. Also, it seemed to provide possibilities for using the recording as a pacer so that rate of reading could be gradually increased. Finally, it allowed for the same text to be available at various levels of difficulty – better readers could have a faster recording which would maintain their concentration, while the poorer readers could have a recording at a slower rate which suited their capacities.

Our first study (Neville and Pugh 1975a) explored the use of time-compressed and time-expanded speech in developing the English reading proficiency of the foreign students already mentioned. However, it was not possible to separate out the effects of the course on the one hand and the students' other English practice on the other, and so this study, though showing gratifying improvement in reading fluency, was mainly of value for showing the practicality of reading while listening with the refinement of rate-altered speech. Also, the lack of apparent ill-effects laid to rest the influential ghosts of many theorists, including E. L. Thorndike who had argued in his article 'Reading and reasoning' that 'the vice of the poor reader is to say the word to himself without actively making judgments concerning what they reveal. Reading aloud or listening to one read aloud may leave this vice unaltered or even encouraged' (Thorndike 1917, p. 332). Our view then, as now, was that 'making judgments' and other aspects of reading with understanding may well require, at least sometimes, saying words to oneself and that 'listening to one read aloud' can help towards a reduction of overdependence on vocalization.

At about the same time we undertook an empirical investigation of the BBC *Listening and Reading* materials. These had not been subject to careful assessment, for the BBC's evaluation relied on teacher responses to questionnaires and the detailed records of only four teachers. In our study we sought to answer three questions: whether BBC *Listening and Reading 1* helps improve reading ability (as measured by a standardized cloze test); whether slowing the rate of presentation makes a difference to any measured effect; and whether the method is feasible with groups of children in school.

The study was conducted in two phases. For the first phase, subjects were 48 middle school children, 24 acting as experimental subjects and 24 as controls (Neville and Pugh 1975b). The children were aged between 9 years 2 months and 10 years 1 month and were regarded by their school as of below average reading ability from results of the Holborn (oral) reading test (Watts 1948). Below average readers were studied because the BBC materials were originally intended to be remedial.

The experimental subjects were in two groups, each comprising six boys and six girls. The groups were matched, using the GAP test, for reading ability, and one group was arbitrarily assigned training at slowed rate and the other at normal rate of recording. Each experimental subject had a matched pair control (matched for sex and for score on the GAP test). The groups were supervised by different teachers.

The *Reading and Listening 1* materials were used for two sessions a week over a period of seven weeks. The slowed tapes were expanded to 133 per cent of production time – typically a story lasted about seven and a half minutes in the normal version and ten minutes in the slowed (expanded) version. The control group continued their normal remedial work, mainly in small groups with their class teacher.

Results from this first phase showed no significant difference in means between experimental or control subjects, or between slowed and normal rates (see Table 3). However, in the second phase, selection for the training groups was more rigorous and poorer readers were assigned to the slowed condition, while the better remedial readers heard the normal tapes. (For this phase only six controls per group were available.) Subjects in the first phase were retested at the end of the second phase, i.e. two terms (about seven months) after their pre-test. Once again there were no significant differences in means between experimental subjects and controls.

Correlations between pre- and post-test scores were generally fairly high (of the order of .6-.7) and significant (p < .01) except for the second-phase normal rate experimental group (r = .23 n.s.). This would suggest the testing was adequate.

27

Table 3 Means and standard deviations for experimental and control groups (Phases 1 and 2) for GAP reading tests (reading ages in months)

Group	Condition	Pre-test			Post-test			Post-post-test		
		$\overline{X}$	SD	N	$\overline{X}$	SD	N	$\overline{X}$	SD	N
1st phase slowed	Experimental	103.82	7.72	11	109.36	11.85	11	110.00	10.29	11
	Control	103.18	6.37	11	110.00	9.26	11	—	—	—
1st phase normal	Experimental	103.64	7.31	11	108.27	11.68	11	112.09	9.03	11
	Control	104.18	7.52	11	110.27	9.50	11	—	—	—
2nd phase slowed	Experimental	100.09	5.54	11	105.64	6.74	11	—	—	—
	Control	101.83	7.68	6	106.17	9.09	6	—	—	—
2nd phase normal	Experimental	117.27	4.69	11	122.27	10.63	11	—	—	—
	Control	118.50	4.97	6	122.33	8.82	6	—	—	—

Note: numbers were reduced to eleven for testing by absentees

Most groups, both experimental and control, showed significant improvement from pre- to post-testing but this could not be attributed to the *Listening and Reading* training. However, it was in the variances that the main differences were found suggesting effects of the training. Differences significant at $p < .02$, $p < .01$ and $p < .001$ were found within experimental groups when pre-test and post-test variances were compared. The exception was the second-phase slowed group. For controls the only significant difference was in the control group for the first-phase slowed group where the pre- to post-test variances differed at the .05 level.

These differences were taken to suggest that *Listening and Reading* helped some children considerably and others much less, a change which the comparison of means concealed. The normal remedial work ensured more even progress.

Now, although *Listening and Reading 1* was in general no more successful than normal remedial work, it was nevertheless as successful overall and more successful with certain children. In answer to our first question, therefore, it did help improve reading ability. In answer to the second question, slowing the rate of the tapes also seemed to help poorer readers, as was clear in the second phase. However, the effect of the teacher here who used the materials for intensive work also could not be quantified. On the other hand those groups whose teacher mainly supervised, with little intervention (as the BBC's notes had recommended), made very similar improvement to those taught by normal remedial practices. Therefore, our third question regarding the practicability of the materials for use in school was answered positively: indeed, it seemed they could be used with minimal supervision.

Further questions arose from this study. One was how to identify those children likely to benefit most, since the difference in variance suggested some benefited greatly. It was to this question that some of the work on cloze error analysis and diagnostic testing (reported in the previous section) was addressed. Then there was the question which we pursued later as to whether the materials could, in fact, be used with minimal supervision. Finally, the optimum rates of presentation required further investigation.

The issue of rate was studied by Neville (1975) with 118 middle school children aged between 10 years 10 months and 11 years 9 months. Those with reading ages below 8.5, an additional eighteen children, were considered separately. The 136 children formed a whole year-group for their school.

The 118 children were divided equally into two groups. One group listened to recordings of three equivalent passages from the *Neale Analysis of Reading Ability* (Neale 1966), each presented at a different rate (slowed, normal and fast). The other group listened to and simultaneously read each of the three passages presented at different rates. It was found from answers to the comprehension questions of the Neale test that comprehension score for listening was not affected by variation in rate. However, for reading while listening there was a significant relationship between comprehension score and rate of the pacer, the higher the rate the lower the score. This effect was also found for the eighteen children of low reading age. It appeared that a rate as low as 80 words per minute for reading while listening was suitable for those of average reading ability, whereas when they merely listened, rates between 80 and 130 words per minute produced adequate comprehension scores.

The question of the use of materials with minimum

supervision was also pursued. Some foreign students of varying levels of proficiency had used reading while listening materials. Several books were prepared with questions of a straightforward nature to act as a check that students had followed the text and to make the activity more varied for them. Recordings were made of the books and the three rates (slowed, normal and fast) were available for use in a language laboratory as part of an introductory course to study in Britain. This work has not been fully reported (though mentioned in Pugh 1976) because of problems from an experimental point of view in isolating effects of the reading while listening from effects of the rest of the course. Nevertheless, comparison of pre- and post-test scores on silent reading showed considerable improvement in rate and some in comprehension. This occurred despite the fact that no practice was given in silent reading (as opposed to reading while listening) and is interesting in view of the fact that speed reading courses rarely lead to improvement in comprehension score but merely aim to hold it constant (see Pugh 1978 for fuller discussion). From this work and from the study of middle school children using *Listening and Reading 1* emerged the idea of having a library of texts and recordings, with the recordings available at different rates so that children could select the rate which suited them best. Implementation of such a library is discussed in Chapter 4. First, it seemed important to examine whether reading while listening materials could be used satisfactorily in a middle school without teacher involvement. Other matters already discussed were also examined and a study made (Neville and Pugh 1978) to test the following hypotheses: that reading while listening produces similar effects on the reading scores of children whether or not the children's reading while listening takes place under careful supervision; that reading while listening is as effective as small-group teaching for remedial readers; and that certain readers will benefit more than others from a reading while listening course.

In this study both stages 1 and 2 of the BBC *Listening and Reading* materials were used, over a period of two terms with below average readers. Two groups of twelve children in the range 9 years 1 month to 10 years 1 month were formed, each containing six poorer readers and six better readers. Each child was assigned a control matched for sex and reading age. The teachers were the same as in the previous study and their differences in approach were now encouraged. Thus one of the groups (Group X) received minimal supervision. The other group (group Y) had strong teacher direction, including follow-up work, oral reading of parts of the text and detailed examination of their understanding. In fact, as a result of this, not only was more teacher time spent on group Y, but the group itself devoted rather more time to reading work. The control subjects continued with normal reading activities.

Results based on GAP test scores were considered in two respects. The two teaching groups (X and Y) were compared with each other and with their controls. It was found that significant progress was made by all groups, experimental and control, during the two terms. There was no significant difference with regard to mean or variance between groups X and Y. Indeed the results were closely similar, suggesting that the materials can be effectively used with minimal supervision.

Results for the poorer and better readers were also compared. The poorer readers showed a closely similar improvement to their controls who were receiving small-group remedial help with reading. Thus the second hypothesis was confirmed. The better readers taking *Listening and Reading* showed a tendency at interim testing and at final testing to perform better than their controls (who had probably given less intensive attention to reading but who nonetheless were regarded as in need of help by the school). The tendency was not, however, statistically significant.

The third hypothesis was not supported, in that significant differences in variances were not found, though at one level the hypothesis is self-evidently true, in that certain children can be expected to benefit more than others from any cause. However, except for the (not significant) tendency for the better of these weak readers to benefit from reading while listening more than the other groups, there is no indication here as to which children are most likely to be helped. This issue was taken up in the study reported in Chapter 3.

USE OF BOOKS FOR LOCATION OF INFORMATION
Although reading while listening may be useful at a certain

stage and for certain types of reading, the sequential style of reading it requires and imposes is not the only kind of reading necessary in school or beyond it. Indeed, as we have argued in Chapter 1, there are dangers in approaches implicitly defining reading as a sequential activity. This, as well as our concern over vocalization discussed in the previous section, had made us cautious of reading while listening. It also caused us to examine another type of reading required of middle school children.

One of us had already been involved in studies of use of books by undergraduates as part of the evaluation of reading efficiency courses at the University of Leeds. A study had also been made of sixth-formers (see Pugh 1978 and for fuller details of results Pugh 1979). A method had been devised for this work which overcame some of the disadvantages inherent in many observational and recording methods when applied to relatively normal reading tasks.

With middle school children, as with the undergraduates and sixth-formers, our policy was to sacrifice exactness of measurement where the procedures or equipment necessary for precision unduly distorted the experimental situation. (This issue, raised in the previous chapter, is discussed more fully in Pugh 1978, Chapter 7 and *passim*.) Also, in addition to observing reading performance on normal tasks, we were interested in correlates of this performance. In particular we wished to investigate how far standardized reading tests predicted ability to use a book. Little previous work has been done in this area, either with sixth-formers or with middle school children, except that (as noted in Chapter 1), there has been a steady and growing concern with study skills. Much of the advice in teachers' books and, indeed, many of the workbooks for children, is based on banalities, unfounded assumptions, misunderstandings of psychological literature, library practice, common sense and little evidence. Regrettably, this seems to be as true of the 'study skills' field as of speed reading. Relevant investigations are in the study of reading flexibility (e.g. Rankin 1974) and in legibility and visual fatigue, for which the review by Carmichael and Dearborn (1948) remains useful. The few directly relevant studies are indicated in discussion following an account of the studies we have made.

For all three studies of middle school children's ability to locate information in a book, the same apparatus was used. It consisted of a reading stand made of wood and specialized glass and placed on a small table. The glass formed the upper part of the stand and by adjusting the lighting it was possible from certain angles to obtain a good reflection of the subject's face, yet the glass would appear clear to him so that he would not be distracted by his own head movements. A book was placed on the lower part of the stand so that a television camera, placed unobtrusively on a rack overhead, received a direct image of the book on the stand as well as a reflected image of the upper part of the reader's face. This image was viewed on a monitor and could be recorded by a videotape recorder in the circuit. The investigator kept a record of certain features of the activity observed and in case of uncertainty could refer back to the recording which, if necessary, could also be played back to the children for comment on their intentions and actions.

Procedure was also similar in these three studies. Subjects were given a 96-page book, *Rats and Mice: Friends and Foes of Man* (Silverstein and Silverstein 1968) chosen because its subject was likely to be of equal interest to boys and girls, it contained a good deal of information of the kind used in topic work, and it had a table of contents, index and running-heads giving chapter titles. Teachers of the children studied considered the book suitable and felt it could be read with ease. Three questions were devised in such a way that there were various ways of finding answers to them, though use of the index was the quickest for all questions. Subjects were given the book and the questions, and after clarification of any problems about the nature of the task were told to start finding answers in whatever way they wished, working as quickly as possible.

Fuller details of the procedure are given in the report of the first of these studies (Neville and Pugh 1975c) of 30 children aged 9 years 4 months to 10 years 6 months who were judged by the school to be reading independently. They were, in fact, drawn from only half the year-group and had reading quotients (on *Reading Test AD*, Watts 1970) from 90 to 134. Within this range the sample was random except that it was ensured that there were six children from each of five school classes in the year.

Results showed that eight out of the 30 subjects obtained correct answers to all three questions in the ten minutes which were allowed. Thirteen obtained no correct answers and of these only one was judged to be using an appropriate strategy for finding the answers. Altogether fourteen of the 30 children were judged to be consistently using strategies appropriate to the task.

The correlational analysis revealed, as had been found with sixth-formers and university undergraduates in earlier studies, low correlations between this task and scores on standardized tests. In this case the number of questions answered correctly, number attempted, *Reading Test AD* sentence completion scores, and GAP scores were inter-correlated. The only significant correlations were between the two standardized tests: this was low ($r = .395$, $p < .05$).

School class had no ascertainable effect on the results, although some teachers had given particular attention to project work. Indeed, the class teachers on hearing of the results and seeing video recordings were surprised at the apparently aimless behaviour of some of their better pupils, especially when contrasted with certain of the supposed weaker children who did relatively well at this task. They resolved, therefore, to pay special attention to this aspect of reading in the coming year.

The headmaster and staff suggested that we might monitor this attempt, which we agreed to although this precluded us from advising on or discussing teaching approaches. Thus the study just described was replicated with matched subjects in the following year. The null hypothesis was adopted that there would not be a significant difference between a group of children who had been taught book-use skills, but had not had a long period to practise them, and the similar group (in the previous study) who had little teaching in these skills.

In this later study (Neville and Pugh 1977) the null hypothesis was sustained; indeed the second group (though comparable on GAP and *Reading Test AD* to the first group and although they received specific teaching in book use) tended to be rather worse. Table 4 shows the results for the information location task in the two years.

The correlation between scores on *Reading Test AD* and GAP was still low, though just significant ($r = .36$, $p = .05$). On

Table 4 Frequency of subjects with different reading strategies

Average time (in mins) per question answered		Number of questions correct	Strategy						N	
			Appropriate		Partially appropriate		In-appropriate			
1st study	2nd study		1st study	2nd study	1st study	2nd study	1st study	2nd study	1st study	2nd study
—	—	none	1	—	6	5	6	8	13	13
6.2	6.2	one	2	4	4	5	—	1	6	10
2.8	3.6	two	3	3	—	2	—	—	3	5
2.8	2.6	three	8	2	—	—	—	—	8	2
		N	14	9	10	12	6	9	30	30

this occasion some relationship was found between correct answers (though not answers attempted) and scores on both the standardized tests. The correlations were of the order of .55 and all were significant at $p < .05$. There was again no apparent effect of teacher variable.

The headmaster also suggested it might be useful to retest those children who took part in the first study just before they left the school. To facilitate comparison, and since almost four years had elapsed, the same book and the same questions were used. It is recognized that there are limitations in this approach, one of which is that the book may be rather young for the children at this later stage. This apart, the advantages were very much on the children's side.

Results obtained for the 24 children still at the school showed some improvement in that 62.5 per cent of the sample obtained three correct answers, as against 27 per cent in the first study. However, 25 per cent still obtained only one correct answer or none at all (as compared with 65 per cent in the original study). It was judged that ten of the children had still not developed appropriate strategies, while it was noted that the 25 per cent (six) who could not perform the task success-fully were not considered to be poor readers in other respects.

Indeed, it should be borne in mind that all the children studied here were considered by their teachers to be of average or above in reading ability, as was largely confirmed by their scores on the standardized tests. It is clear that ability to use a book is not a necessary product of good measured reading ability, that it does not develop of its own accord or 'by maturation' in all children even though they can read well, and that how to teach it requires considerably more careful thought and experiment than hitherto. These conclusions are based not only on the studies described here, which were carried out in only one school, albeit a school with a most enthusiastic staff who cared about the problem: they are confirmed by the work with sixth-formers and undergraduates, again those who are considered of average or above average ability.

CONCLUSION

We have drawn together in this chapter reports on various studies we have made of reading at middle school level. The attempt, using cloze procedure, to identify styles of reading will now we trust be seen in perspective and not as merely of theoretical interest. The reading while listening method, even with its rate-altered variants in presentation, tends to impose a certain style of reading. Some children may need this kind of help in order to develop fluency: others may already be able to read in a style more like that used by the proficient silent adult reader. While the use of reading while listening might con-solidate some skills, there are other areas in which the children may well need help. Among these, if they are to read. independently, is the ability to use books to obtain infor-mation. In view of growing stress on individual work in projects, and of the need to equip children with skills needed for reading after school, the ability to use a book requires much more attention than it has received.

We have not attempted here to give a full picture of reading in the middle school. There are conspicuous absences, such as motivation, interest in reading and attitude to reading, which we have not touched on. We do, however, consider these affective factors, and factors to do with the home, in the next chapters. Another matter we have not investigated is the role of reading in the curriculum. This was beyond our scope in these studies but it is, nevertheless, a matter for concern that beyond the middle school stage there is unlikely to be much conspicuous attention to reading. What there is, in English lessons, is unlikely to be very fruitful for various reasons, including the broad scope of English, its variety or confusion as regards aims, its general reluctance to be 'functional'. These important issues are discussed more fully elsewhere (see Pugh 1980). Our present purpose is to report the findings from a study which arose from those studies described in this chapter, but which attempted to provide a more rounded view of the middle school reader.

3

Better and Poorer Readers:
a Detailed Study

INTRODUCTION

Many of the studies mentioned in Chapter 2 were carried out
in one middle school in Leeds which is in a predominantly
working-class and lower working-class area. We found this
school ideal for research for various reasons. To begin with,
the teachers did not seem to mind our coming in at all times of
the day, and always seemed interested in our ideas. They did
not object when we asked for complicated things like taking a
few children from each class and putting them in the hall for
half an hour or so to test them. The head of the first year gave
us absolutely all the help she could, and even allowed us to
take a little bit of corridor which doubled as her 'office' so that
we could set up our television screen there for monitoring the
children's reading performance on *Rats and Mice* (see Chapter 2
and p.33). The headmaster, too, never once showed irritation
with our frequent demands on his time and his school during
something like four years and was always welcoming. In fact,
he arranged for us to meet with staff in the classes in which we
did our work to discuss our results and suggested the useful
follow-up work that we did with our television monitoring of
the fourth-year pupils. We can only say that it was always a
pleasure to go to the school even though we must often have
been a nuisance and upset the routine of class lessons.

Naturally, then, we wanted to continue to work in such an
atmosphere; but the children, too, seemed to us to suit our
kind of investigation. They were in no way 'deprived' with
regard to the physical standard of the home and seemed to be
well fed and clothed. However, very often there was little
specific educational help from the home although the parents

wanted the children to do well at school, and often told the children this. Generally parents did not take an active part in the educational process themselves. For many of the children, then, the school was the main educating agent. This was, in some respects, an advantage for us (if not for the children) since we could more easily study the school than the home.

The children that we studied were not a sample from all types of schools, even in Leeds, and were therefore not 'representative' of all children of the same age, but we did know a good deal about standards in this school and we had the results of earlier studies for comparisons. Because of this, we hoped to be able to make better sense of our results in the further study reported in this chapter.

One of the more important, if rather tentative, conclusions of one of our earlier studies was that ten-year-old children who scored about 18 or 19 points on the *GAP Reading Comprehension Test* (McLeod and Unwin 1970) *at this particular school* were at a very important stage in their reading development. They could certainly read, but seemed to lack any fluency and ease in practising the skill. We suspected that they were at a critical point, a kind of watershed, and that some of them would cross this and move easily onto the route to silent reading comprehension. Others, we thought, might not succeed but would remain indifferent, quasi oral or aural readers, and never become truly skilled and fluent silent readers. Indeed, we know from the work of Start and Wells (1972) that at age eleven some 15 per cent of children are still at the semi-literate stage, with reading ages of between 7 and 9, and that many do not ever progress much beyond this low level.

Why do some children cross this 'watershed' and some not? Why do some easily begin to read silently while others progress so slowly? We thought that if we looked at two groups of children, one just above this critical stage and one just below it, we might gain some insights into this very important developmental stage in reading – the stage when an oral reader makes the transition to becoming a fluent silent reader.

CHOOSING THE CHILDREN

As in most of the earlier studies, we worked with children in

the first year of their middle school. At the beginning of
October, when we first tested them, their ages ranged from 9
years 1 month to 10 years. To get our two groups, we tested all
the first-year intake of 162 children with the GAP cloze test of
silent reading comprehension. There is not much choice when
deciding on a group test for this age-range (see Chapter 1) but
we had used this test a good deal at this school in the past. The
first-year teachers had found it useful to have results from the
GAP tests at the beginning of the year when they were still
discovering the reading abilities of their pupils. Of course this
was only one small piece of information, but it did alert
teachers to children who seemed to have major difficulties,
and to those who seemed to have few. This information was
very helpful to the head of year when planning the reading
groups which cut across classes. A reading period for the whole
year was timetabled for the first period for four days of the
week and so the school needed as much information on the
children as it could get, and as quickly as possible, in order to
set up the groups. The teachers were well aware, as we were,
that tests cannot give insights into reading development or tell
us what reading level an individual child ought to attain, but
they were useful for our categorization purposes.

We administered the GAP tests to each class, using the two
parallel forms of the test (the Red and the Blue) of equivalent
difficulty. Using two different forms of the test cuts down
'cheating' which is a very natural behaviour in relatively young
children who do not understand why, just because it is a test,
they cannot compare their answers with those of their friends.
The tests were marked by one assistant using the test-scoring
system given in the manual (McLeod and Unwin 1970). The
mean score was 19.3. This figure was in line with mean scores
for groups studied in previous years.

We decided to choose twenty children with above average
scores, ranging in fact between 24 and 30 (around the 75th
percentile). These were not the best readers in the year; we
called them our 'better' readers. Ten of them were boys and
each boy was matched by a girl with the same GAP score.

Next we chose twenty children whose GAP score fell below
the mean and ranged between 10 and 18 (around the 25th
percentile). Once again we had ten boys, each boy matched by
a girl with the same GAP score. We called this group our

40

'poorer' readers because, of course, there were far worse readers in the whole year-group. Our aim was not to study the obvious successes or the obvious failures, but to look at those in the middle, who were at an important stage in their reading development, in a rather intensive way. We thought that by looking at the two groups in a variety of ways, and by comparing them over a whole school year, we might see why some children still lagged behind at the end of the period and why some were progressing quite well, or even very well.

The children came from all the classes in the first year and it could be expected that some teachers would be more effective in teaching reading than others. However, as already mentioned, the classes were regrouped for reading and they also had changes of teacher for various other subjects so that we felt that the effect of good (and bad) teachers on the children's progress would be fairly even. In earlier years we had found no teacher effect, even when we controlled for it, in the studies on reading while listening and on book use. The situation was not at all like that in a first school where the class teacher may have a massive effect on her pupils' progress.

TESTING THE BETTER AND POORER READERS

Although we had given the whole of the first year the GAP test so that we could choose our two groups of better and poorer readers for further study, the tests and materials which are described now were given only to two groups, or in some cases only to certain of the children in the groups.

Reading test AD

It was useful to have results of another group test of comprehension of the more 'traditional' type to compare with the GAP results as well as with other types of tests. As in previous studies we chose *Reading Test AD* which is published by the NFER (Watts 1970) as it is a well-established sentence completion test of silent reading comprehension. There are 35 sentences of graded difficulty and each sentence ends in a blank. Four words are suggested for each blank or gap and the child must choose the correct one. We gave this test to our whole group during one testing session in October, very soon after giving the GAP test.

The next test we gave was the one which we had devised ourselves using the texts of the normal GAP test but in booklet format. We had used this 'booklet' test before at the school as indicated in Chapter 2. We wanted a cloze test of silent reading where the reader could see only one gap and the words immediately before it at any one time. This was, really, an unnatural and restricted cloze test because normally the reader can look at the total context surrounding a sentence or paragraph before he fills a gap in it. We had found it useful to have the results from this 'restricted' booklet test to permit a comparison of the types of errors children made on this test with those made on the normal GAP test and on a cloze listening test.

For each form of the GAP test (Red and Blue) we made a corresponding oblong booklet (one blue and one red – pink in actual fact!) about 75 x 200 mm. On the first page of the booklet the words of the test appeared sequentially up to and including the first gap. The second page contained the words after the first gap up to, and including, the second gap. These pages looked like this:

Page 1.   The car was going too quickly down the hill. It could not _____
Page 2.   when it got to the traffic lights. _____

The booklet continued in this way through the whole test so that, in form blue, for example, where there were 42 gaps, the blue booklet had 42 pages. There were practice examples and while the children did these, they were told that this was a reading game where they had to fill in the gap on each page without looking back at pages they had already done, or without taking a peep at the next page. They were told several times that if they did look back or look ahead this would be 'cheating' and would spoil the game. The test took fifteen minutes (as in the normal GAP test) and we watched the children all the time very carefully for signs of 'peeping'. One or two of the better readers did (understandably) try to have a quick look at another page, but when the testers told the children to stop they did so at once and did not try again to change 'the rules of the game'.

Because we had red and blue booklets, we could give a blue booklet to a child who had done a red GAP test, and vice versa so that the booklet texts were new to the children. We gave the test to the whole group in one testing session, also in October, just after the start of the children's first year in the school.

Reading post-tests: GAP; AD; booklet

In June, as the end of the first school year approached for the children in our two groups, we retested with the group tests of silent reading comprehension to see what progress had been made in the year and whether any special practice or teaching techniques had had any effect. About seven months had passed since the children were first tested, and we hoped that they would not remember too much about the first time they took the tests. We retested with *Reading Test AD* and the GAP reading and booklet tests using the same forms in the last two tests (i.e. Red and Blue) as had been used initially with each child.

Reading test results: GAP; AD; booklet

We analysed the test results in three different ways: first, we examined the relationship between the various test results by means of correlation coefficients; second, we performed three-way analyses of variance (Lindquist 1953) dividing the variation observed in the experimental data into different parts and assigning these to a known cause or factor such as the reading ability of the better and poorer reading groups (i.e. two reading levels) or listening and reading practice (i.e. a treatment which some children had and some did not). We could perform one analysis on both pre- and post-test results for each of our reading tests. Thus we could see, for each type of test, if there was a reading levels difference for either pre- or post-test scores, we could see if the listening and reading practice (the treatment) had affected performance on post-test scores and if this varied by reading level, and we could also simply compare our pre- and post-test scores. Third, we analysed certain of the errors made by the children in the GAP tests and the booklet tests.

Because the chronological ages of all the children varied by less than one year, and since we did not wish to compare our sample to any other, raw scores were used for all our calculations. The means and standard deviations for the three reading tests, both pre and post, and for the two reading groups, are given in Table 5. Better and poorer readers are referred to as upper and lower reading levels since the term 'level' is used in the analysis of variance.

Table 5 Test results for pre- and post-tests (raw scores)

Reading level	GAP test		Test AD		Booklet test	
	$\overline{X}$	SD	$\overline{X}$	SD	$\overline{X}$	SD
Upper level (better readers)						
Pre-test	26.25	1.74	25.15	4.13	18.90	4.74
Post-test	28.15	3.99	28.30	2.77	19.35	4.83
Lower level (poorer readers)						
Pre-test	13.75	2.29	16.40	5.12	10.85	3.79
Post-test	20.85	4.58	21.55	5.07	13.85	3.66

Correlation coefficients

Table 6 (p.45) shows the relationships and levels of significance between the various pairs of tests at the two levels by means of Pearson product-moment correlation coefficients. There is a lack of relationship between the GAP pre- and post-tests at each level and between the GAP and AD pre-tests. However, there is a significant relationship between the post-tests of the GAP and AD showing that the pre-test of AD appeared to be a better predictor of individual reading development during the year (as measured by our tests) than the GAP test. This was true at both levels, although the relationship between the tests was higher for the better readers at the upper level. Even so, the coefficients were not very high.

Table 6 Correlation coefficients for upper and lower levels for tests GAP, AD, booklet (all pre- and post) and '*Electricity*'

Test	Level	Gap post	AD pre	AD post	Bk. pre	Bk. post	El.b	El.e	El.total
						Test			
GAP pre	Upper	.35	.28	.34	.15	-.09	.17	.12	.18
	Lower	.37	.36	.31	.23	-.15	-.15	-.26	-.27
GAP post	Upper		.45*	.68***	.28	-.15	.21	.26	.31
	Lower		.66**	.53**	.52*	.12	.33	.42	.48*
AD pre	Upper			.79***	.19	-.21	.77***	.15	.54**
	Lower			.58**	.40	.49*	.31	.53*	.57**
AD post	Upper				.27	-.31	.58*	.16	.44*
	Lower				.41	.26	.28	.33	.38
Booklet pre	Upper					.48*	-.02	-.01	-.02
	Lower					-.04	.53*	.05	.25
Booklet post	Upper						-.33	-.14	-.29
	Lower						-.07	.31	.22
Elect. begin	Upper							.15	.67***
	Lower							.25	.61***
Elect. end	Upper								.83***
	Lower								.92***

* $p < .05$
** $p < .01$
*** $p < .001$

Analysis of variance

Three-way analyses of variance were next carried out for the GAP, *Reading Test AD,* and booklet scores (Lindquist 1953). There were two between-variables, the reading level and the listening and reading treatment groups. The within-variable was the two tests, pre and post. The summaries of the analyses of variance are given in Tables 7, 8 and 9 (pp.46-7).

From the three tables it can be seen that for each of the three tests there was a simple levels effect in the expected direction; that is the upper level (better reading group) had statistically higher scores than the lower level (poorer reading group). Similarly, for all three tests there was a statistically significant increase in scores between pre- and post-tests. This would be expected over one school year, but the interaction between test and level on the GAP and booklet tests was caused by a greater increase between pre- and post-test scores at the lower level than at the upper level. Thus, our whole group of better readers made less progress than our whole group of poorer readers. This may have been caused by particularly effective teaching of the poorer group but the regression effect probably affected the results since the same tendency was shown also for *Reading Test AD,* i.e. with repeated testing, results tended to come closer to the mean rather than become more extreme. Also, since our better readers already had obtained quite high scores they had, so to speak, less room on the test to show improvement; the limits of the test imposed a ceiling on their progress. This would not be so for the poorer readers. It may be, too, that the poorer readers profited more from their practice with cloze tests. The better readers could already have been more familiar with this type of reading activity when our investigation began.

Table 7 Summary of three-way analysis of variance for *GAP Reading Comprehension Test*

Source of variation	df	MS	F	Level of significance
Between subjects	159			
B (level)	1	2564.21	922.58	.001
C (treatment)	1	24.24	9.06	.01
BC	1	7.20	2.70	n.s.
Error (b)	156	2.67		
Within subjects	160			
A (pre/post test)	1	328.05	28.59	.001
AB	1	76.05	6.63	.05
AC	1	1.25	0.11	n.s.
ABC	1	11.25	0.98	n.s.
Error (w)	156	11.48		
Total	319			

Table 8 Summary of three-way analysis of variance
for *Reading Test AD*

Source of variation	df	MS	F	Level of significance
Between subjects	159			
B (level)	1	1201.25	333.68	.001
C (treatment)	1	0.05	0.01	n.s.
BC	1	145.80	40.50	.001
Error (b)	156	3.60		
Within subjects	160			
A (pre/post test)	1	344.45	57.57	.001
AB	1	20.00	3.34	n.s.
AC	1	3.20	0.53	n.s.
ABC	1	4.05	0.68	n.s.
Error (w)	156	5.98		
Total	319			

Table 9 Summary of three-way analysis of variance for
GAP booklet tests

Source of variation	df	MS	F	Level of significance
Between subjects	159			
B (level)	1	918.01	988.17	.001
C (treatment)	1	23.11	24.88	.001
BC	1	35.11	37.79	.001
Error (b)	156	0.93		
Within subjects	160			
A (pre/post test)	1	59.51	8.14	.001
AB	1	32.51	4.44	.05
AC	1	52.81	7.22	.001
ABC	1	0.11	0.002	n.s.
Error (w)	156	7.32		
Total	319			

Analysis of errors in the GAP reading and booklet tests

All the errors made by the children in filling in the gaps in the GAP tests were recorded. Each error occurring in gaps 1-19 inclusive in the pre-tests and gaps 1-24 inclusive in the post-tests was assigned to one of three categories: whether it was appropriate with regard to the sentence context preceding the gap; whether it was appropriate in terms of the total context of the sentence containing the gap; whether the error was quite inappropriate to the test sentence in which it occurred. This method of categorization has already been mentioned in discussion in Chapter 2 of our earlier work at the school (Neville and Pugh 1976).

Gaps 1-19 or 1-24 were analysed rather than all the errors because a score of 19 on the reading pre-test and 24 on the reading post-test approximated to the means for those tests. Thus, both better and poorer readers had, in nearly all instances, attempted to fill gaps 1-19 and 1-24 in the pre- and post-reading tests. Later in the test too many children found the test very hard and so their errors gave us no sensible information.

From the errors in gaps 1-19 or 1-24, those occurring in twelve 'critical gaps' were considered separately. Because of their position in the sentences, these twelve gaps had been found in our earlier study (Neville and Pugh 1976) to be particularly sensitive to subjects' awareness of total sentence context as opposed to awareness of preceding context only.

Since the frequencies of errors entirely inappropriate to the context of the test sentences were very low and often zero, this category had to be disregarded in most of the analyses of frequencies of errors.

The first analyses were performed separately on errors in form Blue and in form Red since in an earlier study (Neville and Pugh 1974) the frequencies of types of errors in the two forms had been found to differ significantly. However, in this study no significant differences in frequencies of types of errors were found between the two forms and, accordingly, they were combined for the subsequent analyses.

The relationships between type of error (appropriate to preceding context or appropriate to total context) and either reading level or experimental group were tested by means of

2 x 2 continency tables. The results can be summarized as follows:

Pre-test (gaps 1-19)

Reading (forms Red and Blue combined) The better readers made significantly fewer errors suitable to the preceding context only and the poorer readers significantly more errors suitable only to the preceding context than expected ($\chi^2 = 19.08$, p < .001).

Booklet (forms Red and Blue combined)
There was no difference in type of errors for either level of reading ability.

Twelve 'critical' gaps (chosen from gaps 1-19)

For the reading test and for the booklet test, the results were similar to those for gaps 1-19 although the level of significance ($\chi^2 = 4.31$, p < .05) obtained for the reading test, was not as high for the 'critical' gap analysis.

Post-test (gaps 1-24)

Reading (forms Red and Blue combined)
There was no reading levels effect with regard to frequency of type of error.

Booklet (forms Red and Blue combined)
Similarly, there was no reading levels effect for frequency of type of error.

Twelve 'critical' gaps (chosen from gaps 1-19)

Although the poorer readers made more errors suitable only to preceding context than the better readers, this difference was not significant.

Booklet Here there was no reading levels effect with regard to type of error.

Experimental effect

There was no experimental effect on type of error either for errors in gaps 1-24 or in the twelve 'critical' gaps for reading and booklet tests.

Frequencies for each category of error in the two groups for either reading or booklet tests for the twelve critical gaps, show little change between pre- and post-tests. The very big difference between better and poorer readers in type of error (suitable or unsuitable to total or to preceding context) found at the beginning of the school year, had been greatly reduced by its end. This is, perhaps, an indication that poorer readers had begun to change their style of reading.

Beginning-end cloze test

Towards the end of the first term of the school year, we gave the 40 children one more group cloze test of silent reading comprehension. This test we constructed ourselves from a story in the *Ladybird* book *Electricity* (Havenhand 1966). In this cloze test there was not a regular deletion of, say, every tenth or eighth word, instead we deleted both first and last words of alternate sentences. In this way, a complete sentence was followed by a sentence missing its first and last words and this was then followed by a complete sentence, and so on, until the end of the passage. We had 30 sentences and so we had 30 gaps, two in each of fifteen sentences and no gaps in the other fifteen sentences. The children had two practice sentences before they began the test and, as before, fifteen minutes in which to complete it. They seemed to find no difficulty in understanding what to do, but even our better readers found the actual task rather hard.

Our reasons for devising the booklet test and the 'Electricity' test arose from our earlier work on cloze tests and analysis of the errors made in them (see pp.23-4). We had found (Neville and Pugh 1976) that better readers tended to make errors on the normal GAP test that still made some sense in the total context but, of course, in the booklet test their mistakes made sense only in terms of what they had already read (preceding context) since they could not glance ahead before filling a gap. The poorer readers seemed to make much the same kind of mistake whatever the test; even when they could look ahead before filling a gap they seemed not to bother and were quite content to deal with the words (and gaps) in the sentences sequentially. We thought that if this difference between better and poorer readers were important, then our two groups of readers would show differences in the kind of mistakes they made in gaps at the beginning of sentences, compared with gaps at the end of sentences. The better readers would make about the same number in either position and all the mistakes would have about the same relevance to the total meaning. The poorer readers, if they did not appreciate the importance of total context during reading, should make more mistakes, and the most mistakes inappropriate in terms of total context, in the gaps at the beginning of sentences.

So, to try to check this reasoning, we not only noted the total number of gaps correctly filled by each child, but we also had a score for correct words in beginning gaps and one for correct answers for end gaps. Then we could compare these two scores for our better readers and our poorer readers to see if the test would show a difference between them.

Beginning-end cloze test results

The 'beginning-end gaps' cloze comprehension test was analysed in a manner similar to the other reading tests. The total score was determined, as were also the scores for each subject for number of beginning of sentence gaps filled correctly and number of end of sentence gaps filled correctly. The relationships between these three scores and other reading test scores for each of the two reading levels is given in Table 6 (see p.45).

Scores for gaps filled correctly at the beginning of sentences are significantly related (for the upper level only) with both pre- and post-tests of *Reading Test AD* (a sentence completion test) but not with the GAP reading tests. There is a relationship for the lower group between the 'beginning' score and the pre-test of the GAP booklet test. For both levels, the beginning and end scores were clearly related to the total score of the test to which, of course, these sub-scores contribute. The correlation coefficients, at both levels, were highest between the end gap scores and the total scores.

A three-way analysis of variance was also carried out but now the within variable was the beginning and end scores. As before, the first between variable was the reading level and the second the treatment (*Listening and Reading* practice). The results of the analysis are given in Table 10 (see p.52).

A simple levels effect is shown once again in favour of the upper level. There is also a simple within effect which is found to be caused by higher end-gap scores compared to beginning-gap scores. The interaction between position of gap and level is caused by the subjects at the upper level (the better readers) obtaining a higher beginning-gap score relative to the end-gap score than the lower level subjects (poorer readers).

Thus there was some relationship between beginning scores for better readers and *Reading Test AD* but not with GAP reading tests. As we had expected, the beginning scores were lower than the end scores and our better readers got more beginning gaps right, relative to end gaps, than did our poorer readers. This confirmed that at the early stages of our investigation there was a difference in style of reading, with regard to use of context, between better and poorer readers.

Table 10 Summary of three-way analysis of variance for 'beginning-end' cloze test

Source of variation	df	MS	F	Level of significance
Between subjects	159			
B (level)	1	140.45	256.76	.001
C (treatment)	1	3.21	5.85	.05
BC	1	0.24	0.37	n.s.
Error (b)	156	0.55		
Within subjects	160			
A (Gap position)	1	68.45	98.63	.001
AB	1	4.05	5.84	.05
AC	1	12.80	18.44	.001
ABC	1	0.01	0.001	n.s.
Error (w)	156	0.69		
Total	319			

Practising Listening and Reading

As we had shown in some detail in Chapter 2, the BBC *Listening and Reading* materials were studied from several aspects in our earlier investigations (Neville and Pugh 1975b and 1978).We had found considerable improvement in the reading of some of the children using the materials; also, it had seemed to us that the scheme could be used successfully with little teacher intervention. The *Listening and Reading* materials consist of interesting children's stories read with good dramatic effect by the BBC's professional readers, and recorded on tape. To go with the tape, there are individual books containing the same stories so that each child, as he listens to the story on the tape, can follow the words in his own book (BBC 1971, 1972). We used the Penguin Education (1973) edition of the stories as these books are well-produced and have good coloured illustrations of the stories for added interest.

In our 'experimental' school, the teachers used the Tandberg Group Trainer for playing the tapes because, with this machine, ten children and the teacher can listen simultaneously through headphones, and the teacher can use his microphone to speak to any child. Everyone in the school liked this arrangement because a group could be listening without disturbing other children. The children wearing the headphones also felt rather proud of their equipment and one or two said that they pretended they were disc jockeys while they were doing their 'reading'.

When we had used the material before, we had also altered the rate of the recorded story on the tapes. We could do this by using a Varispeech speech compression-expansion machine which was owned by the University of Leeds. This machine discards or adds very tiny intervals of time (around 20 milliseconds) on the tape between and within words. The tiny additions of 'space', or tiny sections of the recorded message removed, do not really affect intelligibility unless compression or expansion exceeds 33 per cent of the original recorded time. Of course pitch is not affected by this expansion/compression process as it would be if the tape were simply speeded up or slowed down.

When we first suggested to the teachers that we could slow down or speed up the listening tapes, one teacher in particular was not very enthusiastic. He seemed to feel that it was wrong to interfere with what the BBC had produced (although broadcasting companies actually use speech compression and expansion machines to vary the rate of various recorded texts). However, we persuaded him to try some tapes which had been slowed down so that they took one-third more than the original recorded time to play back. He worked with poor readers who read the BBC easier Stage 1 stories and listened to the slowed tapes while they read. After practice with the slowed tape, the children could then listen again to the story (while reading) at the normal rate. We had found (Neville and Pugh 1975a) working with *Listening and Reading* materials with adults reading English as a foreign language, that speeding up the tape made the activity harder, although the *content* of the text was not altered. The teacher found the same effect with his young English-speaking children who were still poor readers. They loved the stories and did not mind hearing and reading them several times. Hearing them at the first, slowed rate, made the task suitable for poor readers; when they knew the text better, the normal tape helped them to read fluently at a faster pace. With better readers, a tape at an accelerated rate encouraged them to read fluently but a little more rapidly than normal, measured speech rate. We must mention that when our doubting teacher left to take up a headship away from Leeds he begged us to let him take the slowed tapes with him to his new school.

Listening and Reading groups

From our earlier work with *Listening and Reading* in the school, we thought that perhaps this kind of practice did help children at the intermediate stage of reading development make the transition to silent reading. Thus we especially wanted to compare the effect of practice on our better and poorer readers. Since we had twenty children in the poorer, and twenty in the better reading groups we should, ideally, have chosen ten randomly from each group to have the *Listening and Reading* practice. Then we could have compared their later performance with the other ten children in each group with an easy mind. Because we had to fit in with the wishes of the school in this matter we had to agree that the ten poorer readers who were to have the practice were those whom the teachers felt would most benefit from this particular activity. For instance, they felt that the practice was particularly good for children who had difficulty in concentrating during reading. The ten better readers who used the material were 'volunteers' from among the full group of twenty because the teachers felt that one of the sessions for these children could only be held in the lunch hour. Since these children were, after all, able to read, the teachers felt that real 'school time' should be used for more teaching rather than for 'practice'. Obviously, the children were bound to be biased in favour of the activity and, as well, their attendance at the lunch-time sessions must have been rather erratic.

Yet although our two *Listening and Reading* practice groups, chosen from among the better and poorer readers, may have been rather different in certain respects from the two 'control' groups (who were the remaining better and poorer readers), their means on the October GAP reading test scores were nearly the same:

	Practice group	Non-practice (Control) group
	M	M
Better readers	26.6	25.9
Poorer readers	13.7	13.8

Listening and Reading practice

The ten poorer readers had practice sessions during the first-year reading period on three mornings each week. On Tuesday and Wednesday they heard the same complete story played at the slow rate (extended to one-third of the original recorded time) while they silently read the story from their books. On Thursday, they heard the whole story for the third time, but played at the normal rate. So, in each week they heard and read the same story three times. The next week, they followed the same pattern but with a new story. In this way they read all the Stage 1 stories and then continued with the Stage 2 stories, still keeping the slow, slow, normal, pattern of the tapes for all practice sessions which lasted over the second half of the first term and for the whole of the second term.

The better readers also practised during the same month in the first and second terms, but their practice plan was different and they used the harder Stage 2 material first and then continued with the still more difficult Stage 3 stories (which the poorer readers did not read at all). The better readers first heard a complete story at the normal recorded rate on Monday mornings during the first-year reading period. Of course they read the story while they listened. Then, on Thursday lunch-time, they heard the story *twice* at the speeded-up rate (two-thirds of the original recorded time) while reading the story twice silently in their books. So, although the better readers only had two practice sessions per week, compared to three for the poorer readers they, like the poorer readers, did hear each story three times. The pattern of normal, fast, fast, for the tapes for the better readers was the same for all sessions.

While the *Listening and Reading* groups worked with the BBC stories and tapes, the other children in the better and poorer reading groups continued with the usual reading teaching given to all the first-year children during their regular reading lessons. Some of them at first thought it was 'not fair' that they never got a turn with the stories and the headphones but ten-year-old children already know that school life is not 'fair' and they were easily placated.

The Listening and Reading test

In the past, one of us (Neville 1975) had tried to test the effect that listening while reading has on the reading comprehension of the text (see Chapter 2). The rates of the recorded test passages had been varied so that one was fast (75 per cent of the original recorded or normal rate), one was 'normal' (100 per cent!) and the third was slow (expanded to 125 per cent of the original recorded rate). The passages had originally been read and recorded at a rate of about 108 words per minute, by a certain female reader not unconnected with the experiment.

She is considered to have no marked regional accent.

To compare the effect of the different rates of the 'listening' component on the reading comprehension, it was necessary to have three short passages of equivalent reading difficulty. The *Neale Analysis of Reading Ability* (Neale 1966) is a test of oral reading with three forms of equivalent difficulty (A, B, and C) and each short test passage is followed by eight comprehension questions. So this seemed to be useful for our purpose and, finally, we chose passage 5 (from forms A, B, and C) which is read successfully by children aged eleven. This seemed to be the right level for our children who, also, had the story on tape to help their comprehension as they read.

We felt that the results of this test would give us some general information on the effect of reading while listening, and on listening to the stories at different rates while reading, for our better and poorer readers. We hoped that the test might tell us whether our better or our poorer readers would profit most from *Listening and Reading* practice and whether, too, the practice might help boys more than girls. The earlier work seemed to suggest that boys are more successful listeners than girls and now we hoped to find out if this was true for both better and poorer readers.

The test was given in early November in the children's first term at the school; all the children, of both groups, were tested at one time by two testers. The children were told that they would be having a reading test but that they would be helped by hearing a recording of the story while they were reading it. They were also told that they would be asked some questions about the story. Then they turned up the test passage which also had a large picture illustrating the story beside it. The tester said, 'Look at the picture. The story is about a diver.' (Passage A, normal rate.) The children looked at the picture for about one minute and then the tape was started. After reading while listening, the children turned down the test passage and turned up the comprehension questions. To make sure that all the children understood the questions, the tester read each one aloud and allowed time for the answer to be written before reading the next question. This method was followed for the other two passages. Passage B, presented second at the slow rate, was about 'War in the desert', and passage C, tested third at the fast rate, was about 'A fox'.

Results of the Listening and Reading test

These results were also analysed by a three-way analysis of variance given in Table 11. In this analysis, the two between variables were reading level and sex difference; the within variable was the three tests, A, B, and C. The scores were the number of correct answers to the eight comprehension questions associated with each test passage.

Table 11 Summary of three-way analysis of variance for the Neale Listening and Reading Test

Source of variation	df	MS	F	Level of significance
Between subjects	159			
B (level)	1	20.01	15.25	.001
C (sex difference)	1	44.41	33.87	.001
BC	1	0.08	0.06	n.s.
Error (b)	156	1.31		
Within subjects	320			
A (tests A,B,C)	2	2.23	3.19	n.s.
AB	2	2.24	3.20	n.s.
AC	2	1.63	2.34	n.s.
ABC	2	0.68	0.10	n.s.
Error (w)	312	0.70		
Total	479			

Once more a simple levels effect was obtained in favour of the better readers. A sex difference effect is also statistically significant; the boys at both reading levels had higher scores than the girls. No other value of F is statistically significant. The fairly high F for the levels test effect is due to all the poorer readers, both boys and girls, obtaining very low scores on the slow presentation (test B) but then compensating by much improved scores on the fast presentation (test C). It has been found before that boys seem to be better at listening than girls (King 1959), and at reading while listening (Neville 1975).

The relationships between the three tests at each reading

level are given in Table 12 below. All the ratios are highly significant for the poorer readers and non-significant for the better readers. It seems that the poorer readers used listening information more consistently to help them answer the comprehension questions than did the better readers.

The results of Listening and Reading practice

The effect of listening and reading practice (the 'treatment') on the results of the pre- and post-tests for the three group reading tests, GAP, AD, and booklet, have been mentioned in regard to the analyses of variance . In Tables 7–9 (p.46-7) the levels of significance for the treatment effects for each of the tests have been given.

Table 12 Correlation coefficients for Neale Listening and Reading Tests A, B, and C, for two reading levels

Test	Reading level	
	Upper	Lower
A : B	.215	.634*
A : C	.40	.759**
B : C	.113	.868**

*   p < .01
**   p < .001

A simple treatment effect (i.e. listening and reading practice) was not apparent for *Reading Test AD* (Table 8, p.47). There was, however, significant interaction between treatment and reading levels. When AD pre- and post-test scores were combined, the upper listening and reading group had higher scores than the non-practice group. For the lower *Listening and Reading* group, the opposite was found and the practice group had lower scores than the non-practice group. However, when the pre- and post-test means for each treatment group at each level were compared by Scheffe's method, the only significant $F(p<.05)$ was found for the lower level practice group. On *Reading Test AD,* those poorer readers who did *not* practice listening and reading did better than those who did. On the other hand, for the GAP reading test, when both reading levels were combined, the listening and reading subjects performed statistically significantly better than those subjects who had no listening and reading practice (whether better or poorer readers) (Table 7, p.46).

With the GAP booklet test (Table 9, p.47), the opposite effect occurred. Here the non-practice group (both reading levels combined) performed statistically significantly better than those subjects who had had practice listening and reading. This was a simple treatment effect. There was, however, interaction between treatment and reading level and between treatment and tests, which showed that nearly all the improvement in the non-practice group was between pre- and post-test scores of the lower level subjects (for Scheffe's comparison, F was significant: $p<.01$). The upper level practice and non-practice groups varied little from one another and the F-ratio between the two means of the post-test was not statistically significant. It seems likely that listening and reading practice helps the development of fluent reading as measured by ordinary GAP tests but not by the booklet test (which is, after all, not really a true reading test). It may be, too, that the teachers' efforts to help poor readers in a one-to-one situation concentrated more on giving correct word-by-word responses and less on overall sentence meaning. Thus, our poorer, non-practice readers performed particularly well on the booklet post-test.

The treatment effect shown in Table 10 (p.52) for the beginning-end cloze test is not of great interest since the children had had only some first-term practice before they were tested. The only significant effect was for a combined beginning-end (total) score in favour of the non-practice group (reading levels combined). We were not concerned with this result because we were really interested in the comparison of beginning and end scores for this particular test.

ABILITY TO USE A BOOK

In Chapter 2 we have described our visits to the school in the third term to try to find out what first year children, who are

60

considered by the school and shown by tests of silent reading comprehension to be above average readers, do when asked to find information in the book *Rats and Mice: Friends and Foes of Men* (Silverstein and Silverstein 1968). This book has a table of contents, an index, and chapter-headings, but very few pictures. We had found that unless the reader is very skilled in skimming and search reading, he must use information location skills to answer questions on the text of *Rats and Mice*.

We gave each child the same three questions of a sentence completion type and allowed a maximum of ten minutes for him to find the answers from the book. To make sure he understood the questions, we read them aloud to him before the test began. Then we left him alone sitting at a reading stand which supported the book and also the question paper. As described in more detail in Chapter 2, the upper half of the stand appears to the reader to be made of rather dark glass but it is really a half-silvered mirror. This is angled so that it reflects the child's eyes and the upper part of his face as well as the book and the question paper. The reflection is registered by a camera suspended above the child's head, recorded on video tape, and displayed on a television screen in another room. So, while the observer sits elsewhere, she can comfortably note what the child is doing as he tries to find the answers to the three questions; she can also record what location methods the child is using and the time it takes him to answer each question. Of course the camera cannot record such details as eye-movements but it does show what part of the book the child is looking at, and also whether he concentrates on a certain part of a page, or skims quickly, or flips pages about at random. In earlier years we had been able to note some very interesting reading behaviour, especially since all the children we had tested previously had been so-called 'good' readers. The class teachers also found the video recordings quite revealing because they often asked children to find information for projects, or answers to questions, by referring them to books like *Rats and Mice*. Yet they really had little idea of how the children used the books while performing these tasks.

We really did not think that our poorer readers would have much success with our book use task but we were curious to see if, by the third term of the first year, the better readers would be able to use information-location skills at least as well as the good readers of our earlier studies. So we tested each child individually, using the same book and the same method and apparatus as in earlier years. Of course, by the third term the children knew us very well and seemed to feel quite at ease when asked to do even this quite hard task. When observed on the television screen they did not seem to be at all anxious, even though it was clear that some had no idea at all of how to find the answers to the three questions. Before the test they did not know that they were to be observed but, later, we let them 'see themselves on telly' which was a great thrill for them. At the end of each testing period we also asked some of the children, and particularly those who did well, a few questions about how they knew how to use an index and table of contents.

Results of the book use task

Because this individual test was given towards the end of the school year its results can be related to the reading (GAP and AD) and booklet post-tests given at the same time. The data were analysed as in earlier studies (Neville and Pugh 1975c and 1977). Thus, the number of questions correct (out of a possible three), or attempted, were dichotomized (0 or 1 attempted: 2 or 3 attempted; 0 questions correct: 1, 2 or 3 questions correct) and biserial correlations (r_{bi}) between the two types of dichotomy and post-tests AD and GAP (reading and booklet) computed. The correlation coefficients are given in Table 13 (p.63) for both better and poorer reading groups.

The significant relationship between the GAP booklet post-test for questions attempted was explored further and the results of the listening and reading practice and non-practice groups at both reading levels were examined separately. However, for none of these four sub-groups was the r_{bi} for questions attempted and GAP booklet post-test found to be significant, showing that this one significant effect was due to chance or to factors extraneous to treatment or reading level variables. However, it could be that because of increasing maturity, and possibly some Hawthorne effect, the children in the sample had, by the end of the year, developed a somewhat confident 'have a go' attitude whose effect would be apparent in the booklet test as well as in the number of questions attempted (and thus questions actually correct) in the book use task.

Table 13 Biserial correlation coefficients with associated t-test of significance for book use questions and reading post-tests

Test		Questions attempted (dichotomized 0,1:2,3)	Questions correct (dichotomized 0:1,2,3)
AD	r_{bi}	0.207	0.552
	t	1.304	4.082**
GAP Read	r_{bi}	0.239	0.586
	t	1.455	4.461**
GAP Booklet	r_{bi}	0.478	0.502
	t	3.358*	3.597**

* $p < .01$
** $p < .001$

The methods used by the subjects for locating information and noted during the monitoring of the task are given in Table 14 for the two reading levels. No experimental effect of listening and reading practice was found at either level for methods of location used (and, indeed, we did not expect to find any effect) and so this variable does not appear in any of the tables.

Table 14 shows a reading levels difference with regard to number of subjects with one or more correct answers (fourteen at the upper level compared to two at the lower level). The poorer readers relied heavily on the table of contents alone, while the better readers used the index as well. Six of the poorer readers, compared to one of the better readers, had no apparent method of locating information.

The method of location used by the boys and the girls at the two reading levels is given in Table 15. Although the numbers are small the girls, especially at the upper level, do seem to show a greater variety in the location methods they use. When they found the table of contents unsatisfactory as a sole

Table 14 Frequencies of children using different methods of locating information for two reading levels in the book use task

Method	Table of contents		Index		Index and table of contents		Table of contents and chapter-headings		No apparent method		N	
Level	Upper	Lower	Upper	Lower	Upper	Lower	Upper	Lower	Upper	Lower	Upper	Lower
All children attempting questions	9	12	1	—	6	1	3	1	1	6	20	20
No. of children with one or more correct answers	4	1	1	—	6	—	3	1	—	—	14	2
Average time to obtain each correct answer (mins)	3.2	5.5	2.0	—	3.8	—	3.3	3.7	—	—	—	—

information location tool, they then used the index and chapter-headings as well.

Table 15 Frequencies of boys and girls using different methods of locating information in the book use task

Reading level	Table of contents		Index		Index and table of contents		Table of contents and chapter-headings		No apparent method	
	Boys	Girls	Boys	Girls	Boys	Girls	Boys	Girls	Boys	Girls
Upper	8	1	—	1	1	5	1	2	—	1
Lower	7	5	—	—	—	1	—	1	3	3
N	15	6	—	1	1	6	1	3	3	4

The reading behaviour of the subjects was also designated appropriate, partly appropriate, or inappropriate with regard to strategy adopted for finding the answer to the three questions from the book within the maximum time of ten minutes. Appropriate strategy was considered to be purposeful use of aids to information location with associated skimming. Inappropriate strategy was aimless flicking backwards and forwards through the book with little or no use of information location aids. The frequencies of type of strategy for the two reading levels are given in Table 16 (p.66).

Although both reading levels had about the same frequencies of partly appropriate strategies, the group of better readers had ten subjects using appropriate behaviour and the group of poorer readers had only one subject using an appropriate strategy. The situation is reversed with regard to the inappropriate caregory.

One other trend observable in Table 16 is that as the number of questions answered correctly increases, less time is taken to complete them. This occurs because of the time limit imposed for answering the questions.

Table 16 Frequencies of children using different reading strategies at two reading levels for the book use task

No. of questions correct	Average time per question answered (mins.)		Strategy							
			Appropriate		Partly appropriate		Inappropriate		N	
	Reading level		Reading level							
	Upper	Lower	Upper	Lower	Upper	Lower	Upper	Lower	Upper	Lower
None	—	—	2	1	4	7	—	10	6	18
One	3.7	5.5	3	—	5	1	—	—	8	1
Two	3.2	3.7	2	—	1	1	—	—	3	1
Three	2.8	—	3	—	—	—	—	—	3	—
N			10	1	10	9	—	10	20	20

ATTITUDE TO READING AND READING INTERESTS

We thought that we should try to find out a little about how the children viewed reading and, if we could, of the attitude in the home towards reading. If we had some information of this type then we could try to see if better readers and 'improving' readers had a more positive attitude to reading and a more supportive home than those children who were making slower progress.

Attitude test

There is one simple test of attitude to reading suitable for children of the ages of nine and ten which was devised in 1959 by Dunham. Dunham (1960) describes this scale as 'Thurstone-type' since it contains three practice items, and twenty statements and questions all of the same pattern as:

Pat never likes reading at home.
Are you like Pat?

Ann always likes a book for Christmas.
Are you like Ann?

The children simply answer 'yes' or 'no' to these questions.

As this is a group test, we were able to test all the children at one testing session during the first term of school. Dunham suggests that, when the test is administered to poor readers, the tester should read the statements and questions aloud, allowing the children time after each question to write in their answers. So we decided to follow this method in order to make sure that all the children fully understood the test. They appeared to enjoy doing it, seeing the whole exercise as a very pleasant interlude in the day's work.

Dunham worked out a 'scale value' for each yes response on the test and so, for each child, it was possible to obtain a score which was the total 'value' for all the responses of 'yes' given by him. This score could then be described according to one of three categories suggested by Dunham. A low score showed an 'antagonistic' attitude, a medium score indicated an 'indifferent' attitude, and a high score an 'eager' attitude to reading.

Results of attitude test

The subjects' attitude to reading as measured by the Dunham scale given in the first term of the school year is interpreted by means of a numerical score. The means and variances for the two reading groups, for the boys and for the girls, and for the boys and girls at each reading level, are given in Table 17 below. There was no statistically significant difference between any of the pairs of means, using an adjustment for unequal variances. The significant differences in variance were between upper and lower level reading groups (F = 4.8, p < .02), with much greater variety in scores at the lower level. In the upper group, there was a significant difference between the variances of the boys' and girls' scores (F = 8.04, p < .02), the boys showing a much greater variation in their attitude scores than the girls.

The numerical score can also be used to allot a subject to a category which describes qualitatively his attitude to reading: a score of 8.0 and above shows an 'eager' attitude; 4.0 to 7.9 an 'indifferent' attitude; 3.9 and below an 'antagonistic' attitude. No subject was classed as antagonistic. The relationships

Table 17 Means and standard deviations for results of the Dunham attitude test for boys and girls and two reading levels

	Level		Sex		Sex and level			
	Upper	Lower	Boys	Girls	Upper		Lower	
					Boys	Girls	Boys	Girls
$\overline{X}$	7.72	7.38	7.30	7.79	7.44	8.00	7.17	7.59
SD	1.01	2.40	1.34	0.80	1.33	0.47	1.42	1.02

Table 18 Frequencies of children at each reading level in two reading attitude categories

Attitude	Upper level	Lower level
Eager	12	8
Indifferent	8	12

$x^2 = 1.6$ (n.s.)

between the frequencies of subjects in the indifferent and eager categories at the two reading levels are compared by means of a 2 x 2 table in Table 18; the test of significance gives a χ^2 of 1.6 which is not significant. There was also no sex difference in frequencies of categories at either reading level.

Although more poorer readers showed an indifferent attitude, and fewer an eager attitude than the better readers, these differences were not statistically significant.

Structured interview

By the end of the first school term, the children were beginning to know us quite well and so we decided to conduct a structured interview with each child. We used a list of questions based on a questionnaire used by one of us (Pugh 1969 and 1971) with thirteen to fourteen year-old children. The answers to these questions had been useful in gaining some information about children's reading interests and so we modified the questionnaire a little to make it more suitable for younger children, and then administered it individually. We asked each child the same questions, although not necessarily in the same order, since we wanted the interview to be as 'natural' and as informal and friendly as possible. This was, of course, fairly easy to achieve since we knew the children well by sight. Each interview took about fifteen minutes.

Some questions were framed to try to find out the type and quality of each child's leisure reading as well as the popularity of reading compared with other leisure time activities such as watching television, playing sports, dancing, listening to pop music or talking to a friend. Other questions tried to find out the importance given, in the home generally, to reading and a little about the quality of the home life. Questions to explore this subject are not easy to devise and one that we used, which asked whether the home contained such items as a piano, lawn mower, television, tape recorder, car, washing machine and the like, upset one parent. He complained to the headmaster that he was afraid that the information might be used to plan burglaries – not by the school, but by some other sinister agency. A question which provided us with some very interesting answers asked the children whether or not they thought reading was important.

Some of the interview questions thus gave us information about attitudes to add to, or compare with, the 'test' results from the *Dunham Attitude to Reading Scale*.

Results of the interview

Certain of the answers in the interview were numerical or could be given numerical codings. One question giving a numerical result asked subjects how many of ten amenities listed were in their own homes. The means and standard deviations for the better and poorer readers were:

	M	SD
Better readers	6.25	1.58
Poorer readers	6.50	1.24

So, in number of items which could be considered to be indicative of the material comfort of the homes, there was little difference between the two groups.

Similar results were found for a question asking how many places outside the home had been visited in the year (out of a maximum of ten). The results for each reading group are as follows:

	M	SD
Better readers	5.4	1.35
Poorer readers	5.8	1.64

Again there is no significant difference between the groups.

The children were also asked how many books they had read in the past month during their leisure time. However, we thought that the answers were unreliable because of a great variation in the numbers given. Two boys in the poorer readers group stated that they had read fifty books, as did one boy among the better readers. One boy in the group of poorer readers said, on the other hand, that he had read no books at all. Even if these extreme values are omitted, the numbers quoted by the subjects still range from 1-25. The subjects seemed, in many cases, to have little idea of how many books they had read and tried, therefore, to 'think of a number' that they hoped might please or impress the interviewer. Because of this, the results for this question were not analysed any further.

In another question the subjects were asked simply whether or not they read comics. Only four subjects said that they did not. Two of these (a boy and a girl) were from the group of better readers and two (both boys) were poorer readers so that, again, there was no numerical difference between the two groups. Further study of the interview papers of the four children appeared to show that the two children in the better reader group genuinely did not like comics. Of the two boys in the poorer readers group, one seemed to be denied comics by his parents who appeared to take a very serious view of reading and of the boy's reading material; the other boy did not read anything. The *News of the World* was the only reading material he referred to by name during the interview.

The children were asked whether they liked the books given to them to read in school 'not at all', 'sometimes', 'very often', or 'always' and their answers were coded from 3 (always) to 0 (not at all). They liked the books from school quite well and none gained a rank of 0. Fewer gave a rank 1 than a rank 2, and the highest frequency was found for rank 3.

Two 3 x 2 tables, one by rank and reading level and the other by rank and sex difference, were analysed. The x^2s were 0.14 and 0.15 respectively. In neither case was the x^2 significant, showing once again no difference between the reading groups in their attitude to the school books and also no difference in attitude between boys and girls.

A further question asked the children to rank reading with other leisure activities in order of preference (1-8). Reading did not rank particularly high but there was a good spread of interest, sixteen subjects placing it in second or third rank, sixteen placing it fourth or fifth, and seven placing it sixth or seventh in rank. One subject placed it eighth. Contingency tables were used to compare the frequencies of ranks, first for the two reading groups, and second for boys and girls. Once again the x^2 for each table is not significant showing that the popularity of reading as a leisure time activity was the same for the better and poorer readers and for boys and girls.

A final question asked the subjects if they thought reading

was important and, if so, why. Only two subjects (both poorer readers) categorically stated that reading was not important although five thought that it was sometimes important. Three of these were better readers and two were from the poorer readers group. For those that answered that reading was important, only one subject (a better reader) gave a reason that indicated pleasure in reading. ('It's easy and good to read comics and good to read for a hobby.') For the remainder, the reason for the importance of reading tended to be strictly utilitarian:

> Reading helps you to learn better and if you see a word a lot of times it helps spelling.

> It helps you get a job.

> If you can't read, you can't spell or do owt. Me mam can't spell much.

> You need to read to learn big words but I don't know why grown-ups do it.

> You need to read speeches if you become famous and read letters.

> It's important for your education (the teacher told us that).

> You need it for work. An air hostess or a teacher has to read out things.

> It learns you about all things you need to know when you grow up.

These reasons recurred many times and indicated that the subjects had, perhaps, a more practical view of the need to learn to read than their teachers realized.

In comparing reading levels or experimental treatment with regard to the information in the questionnaires there appears to be little difference between groups in attitudes to and interest in reading. There was, perhaps, a little less interest in reading and more variability in attitude to reading amongst the poorer readers, which would hardly be surprising in view of their more limited skill, but the impression gained from the structured interview is of surprising homogeneity in material comfort, interest in school displayed by the parents, type of reading material in the home, access to reading material and the attitudes of the subjects both to school and to reading and reading material.

These results are confirmed by Alexander and Filler (1976) who point out that positive relationships between reading achievement and socio-economic status cannot be assumed. Pugh also concluded (1971, p.10), 'Surprisingly, it appears that the relationship between positive attitudes to reading, amount of reading undertaken and measured reading ability is less obvious than one would expect.' Possibly investigations such as our book use task, indicate that reading is really a multi-faceted skill. Thus a simple relationship between reading ability and home background, reading interests and habits, attitude to reading, and even reading tests themselves, cannot be assumed.

SOME OF THE POORER READERS

Over the school year, the two groups of readers did retain their positions relative to each other but some of the poorer readers greatly improved during the period (see means and variances in Table 5, p.44). In the GAP post-test, one subject gained a score higher than the mean for the same test for the better readers group and, in all, nine children gained scores higher than the lowest score in the better group (see Table 7, p.46).

Since we were especially concerned with the development in skill at this important stage of reading, we looked in some detail at the results of these individual children to try to discover why they had improved more than the other children of the poorer group.

The questionnaire and attitude scale reveal no differences between these nine subjects and the other eleven in their reading group. Similar means for amenities in the home and places visited are found (6.2 and 5.8 respectively). Numbers of books read in free time range from one to twenty; all the children read comics; preference for reading relative to other leisure time activities shows the same proportion at each rank as in the total group. The attitude scale gives four subjects with an eager attitude and five with an indifferent attitude.

The listening and reading practice seems not to be important since, of the nine, three had the practice and six did not.

On the book use task one small difference is found between

the two sub-groups of the poorer readers: only three, or one-third of improved readers used completely inappropriate strategies for locating information compared to seven (or two-thirds) of the rest of the group.

The types of error made in the cloze tests of reading perhaps show some further differences. In the GAP post-test, the nine improved subjects made a total of twelve errors in the twelve 'critical gaps' of the test. Of these errors, six were appropriate to the total context of the sentences, and six were appropriate only to preceding context. The remainder of the group of poorer readers (eleven subjects) made no errors suitable to total context and thirty errors suitable to preceding context. Such a big discrepancy between the results of the two sub-groups was not found in the GAP pre-test.

A somewhat similar trend can be observed in the results of the 'beginning-end' test. From the whole poorer readers' group, eight subjects obtained scores for beginning gaps which were, proportionately, at least one-third of the scores obtained for the end gaps. Six of those subjects were among those nine who later showed greatly improved GAP reading post-scores.

It seems, then, that these nine poorer readers did perhaps show a change in reading style by the end of the school year. It is possible that these children had moved to another stage of their reading development where they were much more aware of total content and of the idea of a complete written message. From an examination of certain of the errors of our nine 'improved' readers on the ordinary cloze test, and by a comparison of their beginning-end scores on the special cloze test, we could begin to identify this changed approach to reading. Once identification is possible, so is diagnosis of problems and difficulties; on the basis of diagnosis it should be possible to devise special teaching or remedial work.

SUMMARY OF RESULTS

Although the *GAP Reading Comprehension Test* was used to choose our two groups of better and poorer readers, *Reading Test AD* proved to be a better predictor of reading development over the year for the whole sample. The whole sample improved in reading over the year but the poorer readers improved more between their pre- and post-tests than did the better readers. In particular, nine of the poorer readers made great improvements in the *GAP Reading Comprehension Test*. The regression effect may have operated here but it may be also that the school was particularly effective in its reading programme for those children who were still in need of definite teaching to help them become fluent readers.

At the beginning of the year, great differences between the groups on analysis of errors in the *GAP Reading Comprehension Tests* were found. The poorer readers made many errors that were suitable only to the preceding context. Similarly, in the beginning-end cloze test, where the gaps occurred only at the beginning or end of sentences, the better readers gained more correct answers at beginning gaps (compared to end gaps) than the poorer readers. But, by the end of the year, the poorer group, on the GAP post-test, made fewer errors suitable only to preceding context than in the pre-test, and was similar to the better group with regard to this type of error.

This was in general true of the group, but the twelve 'critical' gaps that we had found to be particularly revealing when studying errors gave us more precise information. When they were examined for the GAP post-test scores of the poorer readers, it was found that those nine children who had made the greatest progress during the year were also those children who made very few errors suitable *only* to preceding context. They had also made all the errors in the group which were suitable to the total sentence context of the test passage.

In the book use task the poorer readers were inferior in application of reading skill as well as flexibility in approach to the task. However, the nine who had made good progress were shown to have fewer inappropriate strategies for finding information than the rest of the children in the group of poorer readers. Of course it must be remembered that success in using books is certainly related to reading skill and, thus, it is not surprising that our group of better readers was still superior at the end of the year (when the book use task was performed) to the poorer group.

The listening and reading test showed the better readers' attempt to rely on reading skill as well as listening skill in a difficult task. Earlier work (Neville 1975) has shown that middle school children can, when listening, tolerate wide discrepancies in rate of a recorded message but that they find it difficult to adjust to differing rates of an aural pacer when reading silently. The poorer readers seemed to rely more on listening skill with resulting increase in homogeneity and interrelationship in scores on the three tests. The boys, too, showed more reliance on listening clues which was one of the few sex differences found. One other sex difference was found in the book use task; here there appeared to be an indication that girls might use more variety in their methods for gaining information from a book than do boys.

The listening and reading practice seemed to affect the GAP post-test results. The practice group (better and poorer readers combined) had higher scores than the non-practice subjects, but the results of *Reading Test AD* were not affected by the practice. The post-test score on the booklet test, however, appeared to be adversely affected by the practice, the non-practice group of poorer readers obtaining particularly high scores. Possibly the listening and reading practice encouraged a flexible approach to the GAP test and, conversely, in the booklet test the lack of freedom of access to the text troubled the practice, more than the non-practice group, especially the poorer readers. Certainly, the pre-test booklet scores were poor predictors of achievement at the end of the school year.

However, there was no effect of listening and reading practice apparent from the analysis of the types of errors in the GAP tests or in the results of the book use task. Furthermore, of the nine poorer readers who made much progress during the year, three received listening and reading practice and six did not.

Although there is some blurring of the lines between the better and poorer readers by the end of the school year, they still remain two fairly distinct groups. The poorer readers who made good progress during the year do seem to take a less inflexibly sequential view of the text, although the whole group does tend to forget that 'what comes next' in a text is related not only to what has already been read but is, to a certain extent, dependent for its complete meaning on what may be 'still to come'. Possibly listening and reading practice does help certain children gain this insight into the 'prediction-confirmation' aspect of reading comprehension.

Yet, although some of the poorer readers did seem to begin to learn to operate on whole sentences rather than word-by-word, it is not at all clear how this came about. These children seemed no different in their attitudes to reading or in their home circumstances, either general, or pertaining particularly to reading and reading material, than the other children we studied. Yet they not only began to read better, they also showed a rather more purposeful approach to using a book as a tool for gaining information – a skill in which the poorer readers were generally very weak. These signs of the development of independent reading skills can hardly be caused by chance events and our tests gave some indication that developmental stages might exist. They also suggested ways in which they might be identified, and touched on methods that could help to improve some aspects of reading at the middle school level.

4
Ways to Independence in Reading

In reporting our studies we have indicated some of the developmental trends in the progression towards successful silent reading. It is now worth considering, first, how our better and improving readers had come to their present stage. This is influenced by reading experiences in the first school as well as those in the middle school. Second, we should look at efficient advanced reading and how the middle schools can provide opportunities to help their pupils towards developing it by the end of their school careers. The discussion naturally touches on methods and materials for teaching reading, on testing reading, and on the character and organization of middle schools. Arising from this we give recommendations for helping readers in the middle years of school.

TOWARDS READING FLUENCY

As we have seen from the earlier chapters, we cannot state with full confidence what steps the child must follow to move from oral reading to silent reading. We do know that the successful beginner – an oral reader – normally becomes a good silent reader but he usually does so without much formal teaching or guidance beyond the early stages. We normally assume, also, that a fluent oral reader must be a fluent silent reader (Levin 1979) although it is impossible to check his 'silent fluency' except by very sophisticated measures of eye movements, the eye-voice span, or other measurements of minute physical movements in, for instance, the speech mechanisms. Even these are no more than signs of mental activity. Since we cannot really measure fluency directly, we try rather to measure silent reading 'effectiveness', i.e. whether the reader used the text sensibly and successfully (according to the criteria of the person – often a teacher – who quizzes the reader, or notes the behaviour resulting from his reading). This makes the criteria used of the utmost importance and it is as well to define terms.

Fluency is, perhaps, not a good term to use for silent reading. This was a word used to describe oral reading as, for instance, when Harris (1961, p.86) stated that fluency is descriptive of the oral reading of a sentence where 'The words are grouped in phrases, and meaningful thought units are indicated by appropriate pauses and inflections of the voice.' This ability in oral reading can, of course, be judged by experienced teachers who can rate children's reading for fluency (bearing in mind age and reading experience).

A similar use of fluency is adopted by Clark (1976) writing of young fluent readers in the very early years and many successful teachers of young children will agree that oral fluency can be attempted from a very early stage. There seems to be no reason why even such lines as 'Come here!' or 'Look, John! Look.' should not be read with 'appropriate pauses and inflections of the voice' by a child of five or six. Obviously, if all the child's attention is focussed on a word which he is desperately trying to recall, he is not bothering about his intonation or the 'expression' of his voice. Clearly, he should not be in this situation because a text need not be used merely for word recognition practice. Words can be introduced as units, and practised as such, before they are met in text. The presentation and the recognition practice of this 'unit' need not be meaningless, and new words can also be used in very short phrases where only the new word is unknown; but the text should be read for meaning – and fluently. If this is not possible at the first reading, then a second or even a third reading may be necessary. This may have to be done because the child needs to create a 'redundancy of available information', which includes the cumulative context of what he is reading, before he can comprehend (Donald 1980). He needs time, too, to learn the conventions, structures, and functions of written discourse (Donald 1981) at a period when he still may not be fully familiar with all these aspects of speech. Familiarization of word-use in different text environments is also necessary before the child is really confident in his recognition of a word in any position in any sentence (Francis 1977). Of course, if he has written his own text or story, he will

79

tend to read it back with some fluency since he has, so to speak, already produced it once. However, reading is usually performed by one person on a text produced by someone else. We have eventually to teach the child to read a previously unknown bit of language fluently.

In the experiment carried out by one of us (Neville 1968; mentioned in Chapter 2) where complete reading beginners in the first two months of school had rather different reading experiences, the words in the pre-primers of *Reading for Meaning* (McKee *et al*. 1957) were taught out of context. The books were then read in a group situation but some of the children heard the page of text read aloud by the teacher before they read it aloud themselves. Another group read aloud all at the same time but were always told to 'Make your reading sound just like talking'. Another group were first told to read silently: 'Read with your eyes and do not move your lips.' Only later were they allowed to read orally.

There was no doubt that those who listened to the teacher during the first reading enjoyed reading most. They always followed the words in the book as the teacher (the experimenter) read them, listened very attentively, and laughed appreciatively at the comments of the story characters. At the end of the experiment, which lasted three months, only a few of the best readers showed some impatience at having to listen instead of starting, at once, to read on their own. Certainly, when the children read aloud after listening, they really did try to make their reading sound 'just like talking'. Some were very amusing as they read with feeling sentences such as: '*Good for you,* Tip! You *are* a good *dog.*'

Many investigators followed Buswell (1922) in holding that a listening method would encourage memorized 'parrot reading' but others (e.g. Morris 1963, p.110) were convinced that reading after listening was reading 'responsive' to the meaning of the passage where all attention was devoted to meaning rather than being diverted to 'mechanisms of recognition'. Ordinary teaching experience with children in the first year of school seemed to show that children, even with vocabularies of 100 words or more, really had to be encouraged to read with the intonation patterns of speech. They wanted to read in a jerky, word-by-word manner, even when they could recognize the words easily. Clay (1969) has suggested that this is a stage that children pass through as they become aware of words as units both in speech as well as in writing. When they read in this jerky way they are learning to break up speech into discrete word units and match these with the graphic forms. The problem seems to be that some children never pass beyond this stage. Having identified the units, and matched them, the child must then, so to speak, reunify the written message as he reorganizes it into phrases and clauses. He shows that he has done this by applying the intonation patterns of speech to his reading.

If we ask whether oral fluency matters, the answer is not simple. Clearly, for most of us oral reading is a rarely used skill. Unless we read publicly for any reason, it does not matter at all in our adult daily lives. Why, then, strive for fluent oral reading? Its main pedagogical justification may be that its presence indicates that the child is aware of grammatical constraints within and between sentences and realizes, too, that the written word is conveying a message, as does speech, where many of the words are bound and related one to the other, where we have expectation of meaning, and where this meaning is cumulative within and also across sentences. Reading has a communicative function, as has speech and, as we read, although we are not sure what is coming next, we expect the text to continue the message and to be meaningful in relation to what has gone before. Indeed, the reader must keep a fairly unprejudiced view of the meaning until he comes to the end of the author's words, even though there are many clues in the body of the text, as in a spoken message, to alert the reader or listener as to what to expect next.

If the beginner is a fluent oral reader, structuring his reading around phrase and clause boundaries, he will then have some great advantages over his fellows who can still only identify one word after the other in a jerky, translation, or 'word to name' style of oral reading.

From this discussion of beginning reading, the following important points emerge.

1   The fluent oral reader finds the task easy because he knows most of the words. We may use the old rule of thumb (Betts 1957) that no more than one word in ten should hold him up. If he is reading for his own pleasure, alone, no more than one word in one hundred should pose difficulties although this ideal state

is very hard to achieve with readers with a very limited vocabulary. Of course, they really cannot 'read independently' in the sense that we use the phrase about the skilled reader.

2   If the text is read in such a way that it hangs together, so that phrases and clauses at least are bound and indicated by intonation patterns, the child should get satisfactory meaning from his simple little stories. Even if they are stilted, unnatural, not his own language, contain some new (for him) literary stylistic features, and the like, as long as the child is of normal intelligence, he will be able to gain some pleasure from reading fluently the short sentences, restricted vocabulary, and simple plots of his pre-primers and primers. He may find oral reading a peculiar activity but he will do it to satisfy the teacher.

3   If the child finds reading easy and has a feeling of success, he will read more. He will practise.

4   If he practises, he will become a better reader and he will find that vocalization of words is becoming a drag on his reading rate. He finds that the mediational function of actually saying the words in order to associate the oral form with the written word is becoming unnecessary. He may now not actually pronounce the words but seem rather to 'listen in' to the text. One day, when he reads an enthralling and easy book, he will realize that he did it silently; he might not have even been aware of the oral form of the words. Probably he will find that he read much faster than usual. Then the cue of saying or hearing the word, to give the association of meaning to the written form, has become superfluous. 'Cue reduction' (Anderson and Dearborn 1952) has naturally occurred, and the meaning seems to come direct from the text. Automatization of skill in lower-level reading tasks has thus permitted the development of a new stage of reading (Laberge and Samuels 1974; see Chapter 1). Now, if association of meaning with the text becomes automatic, without overt oral or aural mediation, conscious attention to the text rather than to its meaning is decreased and reading becomes a much less tiring, and so pleasurable, easy and rapid activity.

5   Unless the child has very bad teaching or very unlucky experiences at home or at school, he should carry on practising, and gradually reading silently more difficult texts (more difficult in style and vocabulary), until he reads less for the purpose of learning to read and more to gain information and pleasure from the texts themselves.

INDEPENDENCE IN READING

Fluency in reading, as we have so far described it, is not an end in itself. Indeed, the linear and sequential approach required in oral fluent reading will unduly restrict the adult reader and prevent him from fully exploiting the advantages of reading as a medium. In this respect, it is a pity that much research has tended to emphasize reading at what we have called the aural stage (and, of course, the earlier stages, which have received even more attention).

The recent emphasis on reading as an information-processing activity is a welcome one but two points should be noted as cautions. First, we are convinced that the automatization of skill at the earlier levels of word recognition and 'listening in' to a text are essential prerequisites for using the full range of styles and strategies necessary for processing information in reading as efficiently as possible; second, the stress, even among those who use the term information-processing, on reading as an activity as opposed to its functions (such as getting information), often restricts them to models of reading which emphasize very detailed reading of texts.

The proficient adult reader reads in various different ways according to what he is trying to achieve. In other words he uses the style and strategy appropriate to achieving his particular purpose. However, he does this reading in a context and his purposes are real-life purposes. These adult reading tasks have not been very fully examined though Latham and Parry (1980) show, in their reports on preparing functional reading tests, something of the reading demands of industry, and one of us has elsewhere (Pugh 1978) discussed the varied reading tasks required in higher education. Less is known about those in work of an administrative nature who have, perhaps, the greatest variety of reading to contend with, but who may have the greatest range of skill as a result.

The reason for stressing the context in which reading occurs is two-fold. First, simply knowing *about* the styles and strategies used by adults is unlikely to be very fruitful. The reader is a participant in an activity which requires him to bring knowledge as well as skill to bear. The separation of knowledge and skill bedevils courses in study skills and it is a well-grounded criticism of them that they may lead to slavish copying of techniques (which are themselves of dubious validity). This issue is central to developing reading in the knowledge-based curriculum which obtains in post-primary (or at least post-middle school) education.

The second point is that adults know about the types of information sources available to them. These are unlike school books in that they range from clearly alphabeticized or similarly rigorously ordered reference texts to texts such as novels in which the ordering is (usually and deliberately) not made explicit. In between these extremes are structures which are more explicit (such as reports of research or in industry) or less so (such as travelogues as opposed to travel guides). The adult comes to be able to recognize these structures and to read accordingly; however, he learns about them not as an exercise in text analysis but in terms of their function.

Schools are at a decided disadvantage in introducing children to a range of texts and to a range of strategies for dealing with them. At one level the problem is simply, as mentioned earlier, lack of books. More deeply, the school organization leads to lack of a milieu in which a good many different types of books are used for a good many purposes. There are deeper problems and conflicts, however. The subject, knowledge-based, curriculum of secondary education tends to compartmentalize the types of reading which are done in school – not that a great deal does occur (see for example, DES 1979, Lunzer and Gardner 1979). Thus there is little coordination of effort among teachers and correspondingly little explicit recognition among children of the different styles, purposes and strategies in reading. English, the one subject area which firmly includes reading in its brief, tends to stress detailed reading and reading of literary texts (Pugh 1980). Literary texts are, however, relatively little read in adult life and, more to the point, do not lend themselves to being used in a variety of ways.

In the short term, the recent moves towards English across the curriculum and reading across the curriculum have led to greater emphasis on language in discussion of English teaching: in the longer term, they might attain their intention of concerning all teachers with the language they use and require their pupils to use. Thus all teachers may in time, within a coordinated policy, take responsibility for reading development as recommended in recent surveys (DES 1978 and 1979). This requires a good deal of administration and cooperation and, moreover, represents a change in the way secondary education is organized; it also requires a considerable increase in skill and knowledge on the part of many teachers, yet the knowledge as regards reading development is not yet available for easy transmission to those who do not have the need to ferret it out for themselves.

All this might change, though it seems less than likely that the change will come quickly. Meanwhile, it seems to us that the dangers of study skills courses are worth risking if that is the only way to bring attention to the need for reading development in the later stages of education. Some American educationalists, who have been more concerned with this issue than we have in Britain, also take this view (e.g. Otto *et al.* 1980, Pearson 1980). However, skill should not be stressed apart from application, and the model for such courses should be of learning and evaluating on the pupils' part rather than transmission of acknowledged facts about study on the part of the teacher.

There is a strong tradition among French writers on the issue (see, for example, Blampain 1979) that the school prevents and precludes the normal interaction between reader and text and thus stultifies the growth of independence in reading. This needs to be taken very seriously. On the other hand, the need to attain automatization at oral and aural levels (in our terminology) precedes and is essential to the development of independence in silent reading. One need not, therefore, dismiss school reading as did Huey (1908) as an old curiosity shop full of absurd practices; at least, it is a pity if one must do so, since the skills needed for adult reading could and should be learned in school. In the secondary school this involves some major changes if these skills and strategies are to be learnt in a context which mirrors that in which adults read – or at very least does not ignore or distort it.

THE MIDDLE SCHOOL

The middle school, as we have noted earlier in this book, is far less constrained than the secondary school by external examinations with their fixed syllabuses and associated close teacher guidance. Thus they can still have a relatively flexible timetable and organization, especially across whole year-groups. This means that regrouping for reading and for some special reading programmes is possible. Of course middle schools vary greatly in their organization; some see a danger of a *laissez-faire* attitude in too much flexibility and prefer a fairly rigid timetable structure and approach to the curriculum. No 'best' system of organization for reading in middle schools has been identified and little has been written about this subject because little is generally known about detailed arrangements in individual schools. British school administrative systems are quite idiosyncratic, related to local situations, staffing and the beliefs of the headteacher in each school. This is, indeed, the strength of our educational system even though it can obviously lead to some weaknesses or even failures. Rutter *et al.* (1979) identify differences amongst certain London secondary schools in their influence on children's behaviour and attainment. But they do make the main point that schools can be a force for good with a strong effect on pupil progress. Gorman (1980) makes a similar point with regard to the Assessment of Performance Unit and the new tests being devised for reading.

Ten years have passed since Mackay *et al.* (1970, p.88) wrote that, 'Teachers at Junior School level often assume that the pedagogic aims of the Infant School will have been achieved by the time the children come to them.' They went on to point out that junior school teachers often had no idea of how to teach basic literacy skills and that, in fact, the methods of the junior school often discouraged them from doing so. The picture may have changed somewhat now; many teachers of older children recognize that some children cannot read or write very well and they are now also better equipped to help them.

Weaker readers in the middle school

First-school teachers may have difficulties, but they have certain positive factors working in their favour. To begin with, time is still on their side and, since they start at the initial stage and with an unknown challenge, they tend to be optimistic. Then, too, they often have a very relaxed timetable. If they want the children to spend half or three-quarters of the day reading and writing, they can arrange this. Despite the flexibility of the organization in many middle schools, the teacher of those children in the 'second' school who are not yet able readers (either oral or silent) is short of time for teaching and for reading practice. Of course, much of the child's day will be spent in reading or writing, but in a situation where these skills are a means to an end. For the slower reader, they are all too often too hard a means. Because the material to be read in such subjects as maths, social studies or science may be difficult for the slower child, less of it is read and so time for practice is reduced. The child coming up from the first school may be aware that he is not as good at reading as others but, usually, he has had a measure of protection from the realities of competitive scholastic life and often his self-esteem has not been undermined. In the second school, especially if the child is a poor reader, all too often a creeping malaise overcomes both child and teacher. They feel that the task is too great, and that the child can never now catch up with the successful readers. Very often they are right. As we know, in this situation, negative attitudes towards tasks involving literacy, and, there-fore, sometimes the school itself, may develop.

How then can the teacher of the middle school child stop this happening? How can he teach children, with some slight footing on the literacy band-waggon, to stay on while it accelerates beneath them? We should add that even children who seem to be managing their reading well enough still need much help. It is one thing to reread simple graded narrative texts, often aloud, and another to be expected to read, alone and silently, harder and harder texts not only for their story line but also to gain information. Thus, some of our better readers of the previous chapter, 'ordinary' readers by the standards of many schools, need definite consideration and assistance not only by explicit teaching but also by implicit support and back-up from all the school.

Perhaps this help given by the school is crucial for children in the transition stage of reading. These children have a modest sight vocabulary, some confidence with simple texts, and a relatively small corpus of words which they can recognize. It is essential that this shaky hold be strengthened and not overwhelmed by too much reading that is hard, that has long sentences with many unknown words and which is about unfamiliar and difficult ideas or facts. Teachers in all subject areas should make sure that ideas are understood before they are read, and that specialist vocabulary has been learned. But the most important point is that the texts should be easy. The rough rule, as we have said, is that unknown words occurring more often than one in every hundred words make a text too hard for independent reading; an unknown word in every ten to twenty words means that the child is unlikely to be able to read the text without help. All teachers should keep these simple facts in mind when they are choosing or assigning books to the individuals in a class. A child reads effectively, silently, only when he has the capacity to identify nearly every word and, naturally, when his interest is held by the text or unless he is otherwise forced to give it his attention. Of course, a small amount of difficult, close work necessary to analyse unknown words or to help in the recollection of those imperfectly learned can be tolerated, but the effort required for seemingly endless word identification when the text is too hard is so great that only masochistic children can be expected to indulge contentedly in such behaviour. Even if words eventually are identified correctly, the contextual meaning is lost and any hope of cumulative comprehension accruing from the passage, unless the sentences are very simple and short, is unrealistic.

Southgate and Johnson (1980), reporting part of a Schools Council Project dealing with the *phonic* competence of children aged between seven and nine, nevertheless also conclude that the major portion of a *reading* programme should be 'exactly that'. They state firmly that 'continuous fluent reading' without constant stops for correction and explanation is necessary to develop competence beyond the beginning stages.

A practice problem bedevils the older reader. His reading peers are consuming at a great rate all kinds of books and magazines in their leisure time while he plods through a fraction of this quantity or, more likely, reads nothing. Unless a breakthrough occurs, how can the slow starter (and often slow pupil) ever catch up? He has not the time to do so in school and, unless he has very understanding and concerned parents, it is doubtful whether the home will be able to help much. The school must, then, provide enough easy material in school or class libraries for leisure reading so that, if interest is aroused, it is not at once stifled by stories that are too difficult. Obviously content matters too, and it matters more as children become older.If a task has been hard and relatively meaningless for three or four years (at a minimum), it is not going to become wonderful overnight. Ease, pleasure, and interest must be proved to be possible in free, or independent, reading and it will take a number of positive experiences to convince older children of this. Accessibility of books is also very important. Poor readers are not likely to search for books although they may read them if they are at hand and simple to borrow. The Bradford Book Flood (Ingham 1980) which saturates some classrooms with 'non-textbooks' certainly provides enough books to choose from. The investigator makes the interesting comment that she wonders whether, because of the wide choice, children will learn how to pick a book that they will be able to enjoy. In other words, readers need experience in sizing up books and thus those who read little may need some tactful teacher guidance in choosing books. In this way the children's disappointment in books that look very interesting or exciting but are still too difficult can be reduced. Then, possibly, the poorer readers will actually read and practise, of their own volition, in their free time.

Testing

To make the reading task fit the child's ability presupposes a knowledge of the level of that ability. This statement is obviously axiomatic, whether the information is gained from experienced observation, from tests, or from reports from a specialist reading or English teacher. All too often, these teachers may have some informal knowledge of the reading ability of their pupils, but never pass this information on to the teachers of French, science, maths and so on. These specialists, in their turn, may be to blame; they never ask for this information. The results of tests are sometimes available too and, although they are not very reliable or valid as measures of reading ability, they can give the teacher some more information. If a group test is given, this information can be gained quickly. At the simplest level, surprising scores on a test (whether good or bad) should cause a teacher to look in greater detail at the reading of children whose test results seem to be at variance with their classroom performance. The test information may be wrong but sometimes, too, teachers have misconceptions which test results can modify.

Testing serves a range of functions which are sometimes confused. There is testing to evaluate group progress as a routine matter or as a result of some intervention (as in our evaluation of listening while reading) and there is diagnostic testing (as in our 'beginning and end' cloze tests).

As we have argued, there is likely to be a backwash effect from evaluation testing to what is taught and, as we have implied, the tests available for middle school reading are not good models of what a child needs to learn at this level. As we have noted in Chapter 1, there is a dearth of suitable tests for evaluation at this level although, of course, those that exist are better than none. There are no tests that are fully adequate for diagnosis; this lack of tests is really symptomatic of the neglect of reading at this level and beyond.

Methods to develop intermediate reading skill

So far we have paid particular attention to the special help and consideration necessary to prevent weaker and 'ordinary' readers at the oral-aural stage of development becoming antagonistic to reading. We have indicated that testing can give supplementary information which might help to match difficulty of reading material with reading skill. We have also suggested that reading practice is vital and should continue during the school day in periods that are not officially designated 'reading'. But what can actually be done to teach children so that their transition from oral to silent reading is facilitated and speeded up even at the somewhat late stage of fourth, fifth, sixth or seventh year of school?

Our research with GAP and GAP booklet tests (Chapters 2 and 3) seems to show that children who can read to some extent, but who are not yet effective silent readers, do seem to have a sequential, one word after the other, identification approach to a text. Any activities which encourage children to think of a total written message should thus be helpful. The cloze technique when the children discuss and argue about their errors is useful here. When an error is obviously meaningless in terms of following text, this can be pointed out and discussed. Naturally, general discussion about the meaning intended by the author is also possible. Moyle (1978) believes that, by such discussions, a teacher can observe the language and grammatical facility of his pupils. He can also study their word attack strategies and whether or not pupils use all the information available across the total text to make decisions before filling a gap. An Open University Course Unit, *Developing Fluent Reading* (Chapman and Hoffman 1977, p.116), suggests that discussion of cloze deletions may be a useful way of helping pupils become more sensitive to sentence structure. Pupils should be encouraged to suggest a number of words or phrases for each gap and then preferences for word choice (which could actually be the technically correct word) should be aired. This approach has been formalized by the name 'group cloze' by the Dolans and their associates (Lunzer and Gardner 1979). In their method, children may work in pairs to fill the gaps and then meet in larger groups for discussion. They conclude that this is a fairly taxing activity which needs careful handling by the teacher. Nonetheless they, and many teachers who tried out the method, concluded that it offers a 'fascinating insight into the level of a child's comprehension' (p.240).

The position of the gaps in the sentence may also give a teacher some clue as to how the child 'operates' on a sentence. If he fills gaps at the end of sentences with much greater success than those at the beginning, the teacher should discuss the child's initial-gap errors with him. Many errors in early gaps in a sentence would seem to indicate a word-by-word reader who does not appear to think that following context can have any effect on the identification of words (and therefore meaning and syntax) in an earlier part of a sentence.

As we have said earlier, we also think that reading while listening practice is useful. With the 'echoic' experience of listening while reading, a total cumulative comprehension of text is possible, even for the weaker readers. Some teachers will, perhaps, still feel that there is something a little immoral about making reading so easy but, of course, the task is still quite hard for weaker readers since many words are unknown, or imperfectly known. We found that some of our nine- and ten-year-olds read so slowly that the normal rate was too fast for them. When they could follow the tapes played at the slow rate (see pp.53-4) both we and the teachers could not but be touched by the obvious pleasure these children obtained from 'reading'. We were sure that for some it was the first time that they had experienced a complete and immediate comprehension of a whole, genuine 'story'. Teachers are (and must be) such literate people that it is surely very hard for them to realize that when many children read, the experience is totally different from the teachers' own. As we have reported, reading while listening appeared to help some children greatly. It seemed to give them just the experience they needed to enable them to read their simple texts with greater confidence, and thus more pleasure. We can only guess that the reading while listening practice gave a fluent model which the children could not, as oral readers, produce for themselves. But, having heard the model, they were then presumably more successful at reading fluently themselves. This reading can be oral or aural, depending on the stage of reading development of the child. Young children, and weak readers who are still making conscious associations between oral and written words, may vocalize while reading; more advanced readers may not find overt vocalization necessary.

Tape-recording stories is time consuming but many teachers, especially in first schools, now do this so that children may reread, in their own time, favourite stories and basic readers using a tape and the book. Even if they do learn stories or parts of stories by heart, this is surely harmless. Indeed, repeated close attention to text while hearing words may give insights into graphic representation of words and it is by this means that some young children teach themselves to read. Teachers working with older children could probably also profitably make use of listening and reading activities of either a professional or homemade kind. These activities have the advantage that, once the tapes are made, the teacher is 'set free' and the activity is a practice rather than a teaching one. Teachers of subjects other than English could also, perhaps, use a tape as an aid to the reading of textbooks. Schools might consider the possibility of assembling a library of texts and recordings, with the recordings available at different rates so that children could select the one which suited them best. Of course some teacher intervention might be necessary to spur children on from too comfortable a rate. The good offices of a radio station, university or recording company might be necessary to give access to a machine which would speed up and slow down recordings, although these machines are not now very expensive and curriculum centres could, perhaps, make them available to teachers.

Reading for learning

In our enthusiasm to develop fluent reading with full comprehension of sequential narrative-style texts, we can easily forget that this is not the only kind of reading which the adult reader will have to do. To become a proficient silent reader much easy, interesting (and therefore often story-type) reading is necessary. But, associated with a high level of competence is the ability to develop versatility and to read with differing strategies according to reading purpose.

The teachers in the middle school should begin to coach their pupils to this end. They know that their pupils will, as they move up the school, have to use textbooks and reference books to extract precise and relevant information, to record this information in précis or in note form and, very often, to remember it for examinations and tests. But very rarely does the visitor to an English lesson, or to any other for that matter, find a teacher showing his pupils how to use the reference aids in books as well as skimming and scanning to decide whether the book is relevant and, if it is, scanning to find the appropriate section to evaluate and then to distil from this section the information vital to their purposes. This is not the end; the pupils may need help to record their 'distillations' and their efforts need to be criticized and corrected. Then they may need help in memorization techniques.

Obviously there are many skills to learn and, while much can and should be done during actual, real-life study situations in school, there are also the commercial programmes such as the American SRA (Science Research Associates) *Reading Laboratories* and the English Ward Lock Educational *Reading Workshops*. In these, children follow an individualized programme which should be tailored to their needs. This programme covers a range of silent reading skills such as widening vocabulary, understanding more complicated sentence structures, increasing reading rate, improving scanning techniques, and the use of reference skills. Some teachers are rather suspicious of direct teaching of more specialized reading and study skills and believe that this work can be meaningless to pupils and have little transfer effect to real learning situations. This clearly can happen, but therefore to do nothing is not much help to pupils either. HM Inspectors, in their survey of secondary education in England (DES 1979, p.107) concluded that: 'It is a widespread error to suppose that a range of subtle reading skills will be acquired through chance encounters or through the kind of practice usually encountered as "comprehension" exercises.' In the Primary School Survey (DES 1978) HM Inspectors came to a similar conclusion.

A study of the use of the 'laboratories and workshops' is described in detail by Fawcett (1979) in a recent Schools Council Report. Fawcett is positive in his conclusions. His results showed that this individualized developmental work on reading skills benefited children in the middle years of school (aged ten, eleven, twelve and fifteen) very greatly and that immediate gains in reading were maintained and increased over a longer period. Teachers are sometimes rather quick to condemn materials that, to them, look dry and rather pointless as far as content is concerned. Because they do not like it, they do not sell it very persuasively to their pupils. They possibly forget that these pupils are not miniatures of themselves and may be ignorant of many simple techniques and skills of literacy that the teacher has at his finger tips. Teachers (especially teachers of English) are independent readers, able to manipulate books and texts at will, but children, good as well as indifferent readers, need to be shown how to do this. For some lucky children, according to what they themselves told us, parents and older siblings perform this task. Other children never learn. Fawcett points out that these commercial reading programmes do not profess to be the whole reading experience. They merely contribute to it and, although they may have their faults and limitations, if they are used as the authors intended, they are infinitely better than no teaching of reading skills in the middle years.

A formula which, like the terms laboratory and workshop, looks rather technical and scientific (and therefore serious and

94

estimable!) has long been familiar in North America (Robinson 1946) and is also used in the SRA materials. This is the SQ3R approach to learning material from books. The symbols simply remind the learner that when he wants to remember what he is reading he should first *Survey* the material, and on the basis of this overview formulate some *Questions* which should guide his reading. He then *Reads* the text, trying to answer his questions; then he *Reviews* important parts of the material and, finally, he *Recites* or endeavours to remember the main facts from the text. Obviously this is only one approach to what in the end must be a personal matter but, at the very least, discussion of an approach such as SQ3R opens up the subject and shows children that salient facts in a text do not normally leap to the memory and remain there, clear and accessible, without any effort on the part of the reader. Each person has to work quite hard to find what is, for him, the most efficient and effective way to extract and remember information presented in running prose. Teachers of the middle years of schooling should try to show children how they might do this. The Dolans and their associates (Lunzer and Gardner 1979) used the SQ3R approach in a group situation and this provoked discussion about methods of study and recall. One of us (Pugh 1978) has pursued reading for study quite extensively with university staff and students and has emphasized the importance of having terminology for examining and discussing how one reads. Even at this level it seems that help is needed, as was confirmed by studies of locating information by undergraduates and sixth-formers in connection with courses on reading efficiency.

The results of our book use task (described in Chapters 2 and 3) show surprising differences amongst middle school children, and especially weaknesses in those who are shown on reading tests to be good readers, in their skill in finding information from a book. These results tell us two things. First, and most obvious, is that it does seem that most children would profit from help in locating facts and in learning how to utilize the structure and organization of a book in order to gain information from it while reading it silently. Children seem to need to be given much individual help during topic or project periods in a real 'research' situation to enable them to develop this knowledge. Teachers of all subjects should be aware of this need. Second, until a child can confidently perform such an operation as the book use task, he cannot truly be called an independent reader. He may be able to read a narrative silently and with comprehension but, until he can manipulate texts to his advantage and to meet his needs, he cannot be said to be a proficient reader, able to use his literacy in any learning situation. He should be learning to do this in the middle school.

SUMMARY

We are convinced that success, and therefore confidence, are essential at every stage of reading development. The child should not be pushed on too quickly but neither should he be held back when he is ready to move to the next stage. This can easily happen if a child is forced to continue reading orally, pronouncing each word, in a rigid, sequential manner even though he knows each word perfectly and has, indeed, quite likely read the passage silently before coming to mouth the words to his teacher. Of course, as we have said, pushing on beyond the oral or aural stage before the child is ready is equally unfortunate. How then can we identify the stage the child has reached and facilitate his transition from oral to silent and, finally, to independent reading?

First, we must make him a confident oral reader of his initial, small store of words. He must come to recognize them in any context and be quite sure of their unchanging form. This, so easily written, may be a slow and hard task. On the positive side, it is fairly easy to monitor the progress of the child at this stage.

Second, only if the words are immediately recognizable to the child will he be able to read aloud fluently. Since this early stage may be slow, a model of fluent reading of texts may help to show the child what he is, so to speak, aiming for. Even if a little 'parroting' occurs, at least the child sees that the aim is to comprehend a total written message rather than give a word-by-word identification. He realizes that reading is not just sequential word-calling.

Third, to facilitate practice, books are needed, in quantity and at various levels of difficulty. An attempt to match reader and book is important, too, for successful practice. To achieve this match, obviously fairly precise knowledge of the pupils' reading ability is necessary; reading test results can make some contribution to this knowledge but are not enough.

Fourth, the child must continue to practise until he knows the words in a text so well that he no longer needs to make the overt speech association or even to 'listen in' to the words; meaning then seems to be directly associated with the text. But, again, it should not be associated, even though silently, in a unitary, word-by-word way. He must be concerned with total sentence and passage context to gain full meaning and also to help in word identification which will still be important for the young or slow reader.

Fifth, to become completely independent as a silent reader, the child must continue to practise the skill, gaining confidence as he becomes more familiar with the written word and its functions. Some children will read more and more complex literary forms, with varied vocabulary, and novel and exciting use of language aided, one hopes, by the English teacher.

Sixth, at the same time, probably most children need some help in finding out how to use books to gain information from them. They need to examine the structure and style of their textbooks and reference books so that they can assess their value and then use them quickly and efficiently. They need, too, to know how to encapsulate and remember the information given in running prose.

Seventh, the independent reader, which the middle school is trying to produce, is one who uses the written word for a variety of purposes and reads with differing strategies depending on that purpose. Although the reading practice essential for effortless silent reading will, normally, be obtained through narrative material, the proficient reader is a versatile one who must be able to read all kind of texts with a variety of approaches. The middle school should begin to make pupils aware of the necessity of changing style, strategy, and speed of reading as the occasion and material demand. Only when readers can do this are they making efficient use of the written word.

We must realize that some children will not progress so far and they will only read very predictable language structures with familiar vocabulary and content. But whatever the level of the text which the learner may finally read, he should be able to make the transition from oral to silent reading so that he can interpret what he wishes or needs to read independently and with feelings of pleasure and success.

RECOMMENDATIONS

1. There is a need for schools to have a good supply of books of differing levels of difficulty to give suitable practice material for children of varying reading ability although of the same age and interests. This applies especially to books used for studying school subjects.
2. The reading material should be freely accessible so that no child is deterred from reading by the slightest difficulty in actually getting a book. Whether books are in classroom or school libraries is a problem related to the question of accessibility.
3. The use of listening and reading should be explored further, and also by teachers of subjects other than English. The value of altering the rate of the recorded text should also be considered.
4. There is a need for tests of reading which could be used for evaluation and which would, at the same time, assess attainment with regard to stages in reading development.
5. Diagnostic tests which show how a child is operating on a text as he reads silently are also needed. Cloze tests are some help here but they need to be refined in order to be used diagnostically.
6. After assessing the reading abilities of the pupils, programmes should be devised for children at differing stages along the road to independence. A balanced school plan, and one where priorities are clear, is required.
7. Information about what kind of reading actually occurs in middle schools would be very useful. Has it a quality of its own? How is it like or unlike the early reading in the first school on the one hand, and the independent reading expected in the secondary schools and adult life, on the other?
8. More information on the quality and type of attention

given by all the subject teachers in the middle school to reading would assist rational planning for the teaching of reading.

9. Teachers of English need to be better prepared for developing reading skill; we are aware that this recommendation runs contrary to the ethos of the teaching of English and for that reason we consider it all the more important.

10. Authors with our backgrounds always call for more research. Yet without a firmly-established theoretical framework practitioners cannot make sensible professional decisions concerning their pupils that will have a good chance of success.

The middle school is a 'no-man's land' in reading. The beginning steps of oral reading are moderately well documented and we know the characteristics of the proficient, silent reader. How can we help pupils move from the first to the final stage? What happens along the route between these two extremes is still far from clear, but learning to read occurs all the way. It is the teachers' and the researchers' job to try to identify and understand this learning in order to facilitate the child's efforts to attain independent reading.

References

ALDERSON, J.C. (1979) The effect on the cloze test of changes in deletion frequency *Journal of Research in Reading 2*, (2), 108-19

ALEXANDER, J.E. and FILLER, R.C. (1976) *Attitudes and Reading* Newark, Delaware: International Reading Association

ANDERSON, I.H. and DEARBORN, W.F. (1952) *The Psychology of Teaching Reading* New York: Ronald Press

ATKINSON, R.C. and SHIFFRIN, R.M. (1968) 'Human memory: a proposed system and its central processes' in K.W. Spence and J.T. Spence (eds) *The Psychology of Learning and Motivation: advances in research and theory* Vol. 2. New York: Academic Press, 89-195

BADCOCK, E.H. *et al.* (1972) *Education in the Middle Years* (Schools Council Working Paper no. 42) London: Evans/Methuen Educational

BADDELEY, A. (1976) *The Psychology of Memory* New York: Harper and Row

BBC (1971) *Listening and Reading 1* London: BBC

BBC (1972) *Listening and Reading 2* London: BBC

BEATTIE, N. (1974) Reading aloud *Audio Visual Language Journal 11*, (3), 201-5

BETTS, E.A. (1957) *Foundations of Reading Instruction* New York: American Book Company

BLAMPAIN, D. (1979) *La Littérature de Jeunesse–pour un Autre Usage* Brussels and Paris: Labor/Nathan

BLOOMFIELD, L. and BARNHART, C.L. (1961) *Let's Read: a Linguistic Approach* Detroit: Wayne State University Press

BORMUTH, J.R. (1973) Reading literacy: its definition and assessment *Reading Research Quarterly 9*, 7-66

BROOKS, R.G. (1980a) *Normal and disturbed language: the 'diagram-makers' and their models of reading, 1871-1922* Paper presented to a seminar Reading in First and Second Language Learning, Luxembourg, March 1980. Revised version in preparation (forthcoming)

BROOKS, R.G. (1980b) *Suppression experiments and reading* Paper presented to a conference on Reading of the British Psychological Society Cognitive Section, Exeter, 22-3 March, 1980

BUROS, O.K. (1978) *The Eighth Mental Measurements Yearbook* Highland Park, N.J.: Gryphon Press

BUSWELL, G.T. (1922) *Fundamental Reading Habits: a study of their development* (Supplementary Educational Monographs no. 21) Chicago: University of Chicago

BUSWELL, G.T. (1945) *Non-Oral Reading: a study of its use in the Chicago public schools* (Supplementary Educational Monographs no. 60) Chicago: University of Chicago

CARMICHAEL, L. and DEARBORN, W.F. (1948) *Reading and Visual Fatigue* London: Harrap

CASHDAN, A. (1980) 'Teaching language and reading in the early years' in G. Bray and A.K. Pugh (eds) *The Reading Connection* London: Ward Lock Educational, 54-66

CHAPMAN, J.L. and HOFFMAN, M. (1977) *Developing Fluent Reading* (Block 1 of course PE231, Reading Development) Milton Keynes: Open University Press

CLARK, M.M. (1976) *Young Fluent Readers* London: Heinemann

CLAY, M.M. (1969) Reading errors and self-correction behaviour *British Journal of Educational Psychology 39,* 47-56

CLAY, M.M. (1972) *Reading: The Patterning of Complex Behaviour* London: Heinemann

CONRAD, R. (1972) 'Speech and reading' in J.F. Kavanagh and I.G. Mattingley (eds) *Language by Ear and by Eye* Cambridge, Mass.: MIT Press, 205-40

CONRAD, R. (1979) *The Deaf Schoolchild: language and cognitive function* London: Harper and Row

DEAN, J. et al. (1979) *The Sixth Form and its Alternatives* Windsor: NFER

DES (1975) *A Language for Life* (The Bullock Report) London: HMSO

DES (1978) *Primary Education in England: a survey by HM Inspectors of Schools* London: HMSO

DES (1979) *Aspects of Secondary Education in England: a survey by HM Inspectors of Schools* London: HMSO

DOLAN, T., DOLAN, E. and TAYLOR, V. (1979) 'Improving reading through group discussion activities' in E. Lunzer and K. Gardner (eds) *The Effective Use of Reading* London:

Heinemann, 228-66

DONALD, D.R. (1980) Analysis of children's reading errors: a current perspective *Journal of Research in Reading 3,* (2), 106-15

DONALD, D.R. (1981) Learning-to-read: a psycholinguistic analysis of transitional processing *Journal of Research in Reading 4,* (1), 34-42

DOUGLAS, D. (1978) Gain in reading proficiency in English as a foreign language measured by three cloze scoring procedures *Journal of Research in Reading 1,* (1), 67-73

DOWNING, J. (1979) *Reading and Reasoning* Edinburgh: Chambers

DUKER, S. (1974) *Time Compressed Speech: an anthology and bibliography in three volumes* Metuchen, N.J. : Scarecrow Press

DUNHAM, J. (1959) *The Effects of Remedial Education on Young Children's Reading Ability and Attitude to Reading* University of Manchester: unpublished M.Ed. thesis

DUNHAM, J. (1960) The effects of remedial education on young children's reading ability and attitude to reading *British Journal of Educational Psychology 30,* 173-5

EDFELDT, A.W. (1959) *Silent Speech and Silent Reading* Stockholm: Almqvist and Wiksell

EDUCATIONAL PUBLISHERS' ASSOCIATION (1980) *A Guide to Schoolbook Spending in the North-West* London: EPC

FARR, R. (1969) *Reading: what can be measured?* Newark, Delaware: International Reading Association

FAWCETT, R. (1979) 'Reading laboratories' in E. Lunzer and K. Gardner (eds) *The Effective Use of Reading* London: Heinemann, 193-227

FERGUSON, C.A. (1971) 'Contrasting patterns of literacy in a multilingual nation' in W.H. Whiteley (ed.) *Language Use and Social Change: problems of multilingualism with special reference to East Africa* Oxford: Oxford University Press, 234-53

FRANCIS, H. (1977) Symposium: reading abilities and disabilities. Children's strategies in learning to read *British Journal of Educational Psychology 47,* 117-25

FRIES, C.C. (1963) *Linguistics and Reading* New York: Holt, Rinehart and Winston

GEYER, T.J. (1972) Comprehensive and partial models related to the reading process *Reading Research Quarterly 7,* 541-87

GIBSON, E.J. (1972) 'Reading for some purpose' in J.E.

Kavanagh and I.G. Mattingly (eds) *Language by Ear and by Eye* Cambridge, Mass.: MIT Press

GIBSON, E.J. and LEVIN, H. (1975) *The Psychology of Reading* Cambridge, Mass.: MIT Press

GODFREY THOMSON UNIT (1980) (2nd edn) *Edinburgh Reading Tests, Stage 2* London: Hodder and Stoughton

GOLDSTROM, J.M. (1972) *The Social Content of Education, 1808-70: a study of the working-class school reader in England and Ireland* Shannon: Irish University Press

GOODMAN, K.S. (1968) 'The psycholinguistic nature of the reading process' in K.S. Goodman (ed.) *The Psycholinguistic Nature of the Reading Process* Detroit: Wayne State University Press, 15-26

GOODMAN, K.S. (1969) Analysis of oral reading miscues: applied psycholinguistics *Reading Research Quarterly 5,* 9-30

GORMAN, T. (1979) 'Monitoring of language performance in the schools of England and Wales' in D. Thackray (ed.) *Growth in Reading* London: Ward Lock Educational, 234-39

GORMAN, T. (1980) *Developments in language assessment: a report on the national monitoring project* Paper presented to 17th Annual Conference, United Kingdom Reading Association, Warwick, July-August, 1980

HARRIS, A.J. (1961) *How to Increase Reading Ability* New York: Macmillan

HAVENHAND, I. and HAVENHAND, J. (1966) *Electricity* Loughborough: Wills and Hepworth

HEATON, J.B. (1975) *Writing English Language Tests* London: Longman

HERRING, J. (1978) *Teaching Library Skills in Schools* Windsor: NFER

HUEY, E.B. (1908) *The Psychology and Pedagogy of Reading* New York: Macmillan (reprinted 1968, Cambridge, Mass.: MIT Press)

INGHAM, J. (1980) 'Recording children's responses to books in the Bradford Book Flood Experiment' in G. Bray and A.K. Pugh (eds) *The Reading Connection* London: Ward Lock Educational, 122-34

JONES, H.A. and CHARNLEY, A.H. (1978) *Adult Literacy: a study of its impact* Leicester: National Institute of Adult Education

KING, W.H. (1959) An experimental investigation into the

relative merits of listening and reading comprehension for boys and girls *British Journal of Educational Psychology 29,* 42-49

KYLE, J.G. (1980) Reading development of deaf children *Journal of Research in Reading 3,* (2), 86-97

LABERGE, D. and SAMUELS, S.J. (1974) Toward a theory of automatic information processing in reading *Cognitive Psychology 6,* 293-323, given in Singer and Ruddell (1976)*q.v.,* 548-79

LATHAM, W. and PARRY, O. (1980) Functional reading and the schools: a progress report *Journal of Research in Reading 3, (2),* 140-9

LEFEVRE, C.A. (1964) *Linguistics and the Teaching of Reading* New York: McGraw Hill

LEVIN, H. (1979) *The Eye-Voice Span* Cambridge, Mass.:MIT Press

LEVY-SCHOEN, A. and O'REGAN, K. (1979) 'The control of eye-movements in reading' in P.A. Kolers, M.E. Wrolstad and H. Bouma (eds) *Processing of Visible Language 1* New York: Plenum Press, 7-48

LINDQUIST, E.F. (1953) *Design and Analysis of Experiments in Psychology and Education* Boston: Houghton Mifflin

LUNZER, E. and GARDNER, K. (1979, eds) *The Effective Use of Reading* London: Heinemann

LUNZER, E., WAITE, M. and DOLAN, T. (1979) 'Comprehension and comprehension tests' in E. Lunzer and K. Gardner (eds) *The Effective Use of Reading* London: Heinemann, 37-71

MAAS-DE BROUWER, T.A. and SAMSON SLUITER, D.M.M. (1978) Some remarks about the testing of reading a foreign language *Reading 12,* (3), 31-5

MARSHALL, N. and GLOCK, M.D. (1978) Comprehension of connected discourse: a study into the relationships between the structure of text and information recalled *Reading Research Quarterly 14,* (1), 10-56

MACKAY, D., THOMPSON, B. and SCHAUB, P. (1970) *Breakthrough to Literacy* (Teachers' manual *The Theory and Practice of Teaching Initial Reading and Writing)* London: Longman

McKEE, P.M. *et al.* (1957) *Reading for Meaning Readers* Boston: Houghton Mifflin

McKENNA, M.C. and ROBINSON, R.D. (1980) *An Introduction*

to the Cloze Procedure – an annotated bibliography (revised edition) Newark, Delaware: International Reading Association

McLEOD, J.and ANDERSON, J. (1973) *GAPADOL Reading Comprehension Test* London: Heinemann

McLEOD, J. and UNWIN, D. (1970) *GAP Reading Comprehension Test* London: Heinemann

MERRITT, J. (1970) 'The intermediate skills' in K. Gardner (ed.) *Reading Skills: Theory and Practice* London: Ward Lock Educational, 42-63

MORRIS, J.M. (1966) *Standards and Progress in Reading* Slough: NFER

MORRIS, R. (1963) *Success and Failure in Learning to Read* London: Oldbourne (new edition 1973, Harmondsworth: Penguin)

MORTON, J. (1979) 'The logogen model and othographic structure' in U. Frith (ed.) *Cognitive Processes in Spelling* London: Academic Press, 117-34

MOYLE, D. (1978) 'Assessment and diagnosis' in D. Moyle (ed.) *Perspectives on Adult Literacy* (United Kingdom Reading Association, Occasional Publication.) Ormskirk, Lancs.: UKRA, 53-65

NEALE, M.D. (1966) (2nd edn.) *Neale Analysis of Reading Ability* London: Macmillan

NEVILLE, M.H. (1968) The effects of oral and echoic responses in beginning reading *Journal of Educational Psychology 59,* 362-9

NEVILLE, M.H. (1975) Effectiveness of rate of aural message on reading and listening *Educational Research 18,* (1), 37-43

NEVILLE, M.H. and PUGH, A.K. (1974) Context in reading and listening: a comparison of children's errors in cloze tests *British Journal of Educational Psychology 44,* 224-32

NEVILLE, M.H. and PUGH, A. K. (1975a) An exploratory study of the application of time-compressed and time-expanded speech in the development of the English reading proficiency of foreign students *English Language Teaching Journal 29,* (4), 320-9

NEVILLE, M.H. and PUGH, A.K. (1975b) 'An empirical study of the reading while listening method' in D. Moyle (ed.) *Reading: What of the Future?* London: Ward Lock Educational, 95-106

NEVILLE, M.H. and PUGH, A.K. (1975c) Reading ability

and ability to use a book: a study of middle school children *Reading 9,* (3), 23-31

NEVILLE, M.H. and PUGH, A.K. (1976) Context in reading and listening: variations in approach to cloze tasks *Reading Research Quarterly 12,* (1), 13-31

NEVILLE, M.H. and PUGH, A.K. (1977) Ability to use a book: further studies of middle school children *Reading 11,* (3), 13-22

NEVILLE, M.H. and PUGH, A.K. (1978) Reading while listening: the value of teacher involvement *English Language Teaching Journal 33,* 45-50

OTTO, W., WHITE, S. and CAMPERELL, K. (1980) Text comprehension research to classroom application: developing an instructional technique *Reading Psychology 1,* (3), 184-91

PEARSON, P.D. (1980) *Comprehension of text structure, a twenty-year history* Paper presented to 17th Annual Conference, United Kingdom Reading Association, Warwick July-August, 1980

PENGUIN EDUCATION (1973) *Listening and Reading, Stage 1 and Stage 2* Harmondsworth: Penguin Education (revised version of BBC 1971, 1972, *q.v.*)

POTTER, F. (1980) Miscue analysis: a cautionary note *Journal of Research in Reading 3,* (2), 116-28

PUGH, A.K. (1969) Some neglected aspects of reading in the secondary school *Reading 3,* (3), 3-10

PUGH, A.K. (1971) Secondary school reading: obstacles to profit and delight *Reading 5,* (1), 6-13

PUGH, A.K. (1976) *Approaches to developing effective adult reading* Paper presented to the Fourth International Congress of the International Association for Applied Linguistics, Stuttgart, August 1975 *Modern English Journal 7,* 9-15

PUGH, A.K. (1978) *Silent Reading: an introduction to its study and teaching* London: Heinemann

PUGH, A.K. (1979) 'Styles and strategies in adult silent reading' in P.A. Kolers, M. Wrolstad and H. Bouma (eds) *Processing of Visible Language 1,* 431-43

PUGH, A.K. (1980) 'Reading and the teaching of English' in G. Bray and A.K. Pugh (eds) *The Reading Connection* London: Ward Lock Educational, 2-15

PUGH, A.K. (1981a) 'Construction and reconstruction of text' in L.J. Chapman (ed.) *The Reader and the Text* London: Heinemann 70-80

PUGH, A.K. (1981b) *The Teaching of English in Modern England* (Block 3, Part IIb of Course E263 *Language in Use*) Milton Keynes: Open University Press

PUMFREY, P. D. (1976) *Reading: tests and assessment techniques* London: Hodder and Stoughton

RANKIN, E. F. (1974) *The Measurement of Reading Flexibility* Newark, Delaware: International Reading Association

REID, J. F. (1972) 'Children's comprehension of syntactic features found in some extension readers' in J.F. Reid (ed.) *Reading: Problems and Practices* London: Ward Lock Educational, 394-403

ROBINSON, F.P. (1946) (revised edn.) *Effective Study* New York: Harper

ROSS, A.M., RAZZELL, A.G. and BADCOCK, E.H. (1975) *The Curriculum in the Middle Years* (Schools Council Working Paper no. 55) London: Evans/Methuen Educational

RUTTER, M *et al.* (1979) *Fifteen Thousand Hours* London: Open Books

SEYMOUR, P. H. K. (1979) *Human Visual Cognition* London: Collier Macmillan

SHANNON, C. E. (1948) *A Mathematical Theory of Communication* Bell Telephone System, Monograph B-1598, Technical Publications. Extract given in R. C. Oldfield and J. C. Marshall (eds) *Language* (Penguin Modern Psychology Readings) Harmondsworth: Penguin, 1968, 257-62

SILVERSTEIN, A. and SILVERSTEIN, V. (1968) *Rats and Mice: friends and foes of man* Glasgow: Blackie

SINGER, H. and RUDDELL, R. B. (1976, eds) (2nd edn) *Theoretical Models and Processes of Reading* Newark, Delaware: International Reading Association

SMITH, F. (1971) *Understanding Reading: a psycholinguistic analysis of reading and learning to read* New York: Holt, Rinehart and Winston

SMITH, F. (1973) *Psycholinguistics and Reading* New York: Holt, Rinehart and Winston

SOKOLOV, A. N. (1968) *Inner Speech and Thought* Moscow: Presveshchenie Press (trans. G. T. Onischenko, New York: Plenum Press, 1972)

SOUTHGATE BOOTH, V. and JOHNSON S. (1980) 'The

phonic competencies of children aged seven to nine years' in G. Bray and A. K. Pugh (eds) *The Reading Connection* London: Ward Lock Educational, 112-21

START, K. B. and WELLS, B. K. (1972) *The Trend of Reading Standards* Windsor: NFER

STUBBS, M. (1980) *Language and Literacy: the sociolinguistics of reading and writing* London: Routledge and Kegan Paul

TAYLOR, W.L. (1953) Cloze procedure: a new tool for measuring readability *Journalism Quarterly 30,* 415-33

THOMSON, M. (1978) A psycholinguistic analysis of reading errors made by dyslexics and normal readers *Journal of Research in Reading 1,* (1), 7-20

THORNDIKE, E. L. (1917) Reading as reasoning: a study of mistakes in paragraph reading *Journal of Educational Psychology 8,* 323-32

TIERNEY, R.J. and MOSENTHAL, J. (1980) *Discourse Comprehension and Production: analyzing text structure and cohesion* Technical Report no. 152, Center for the Study of Reading, University of Illinois at Urbana-Champaign

ULIJN, J. (1980) Foreign language reading research: recent trends and future prospects *Journal of Research in Reading 3,* (1), 17-37

WALKER, C. (1974) *Reading Development and Extension* London: Ward Lock Educational

WATTS, A. F. (1948) *Holborn Reading Scale* London: Harrap

WATTS, A. F. (1970) *Reading Test AD* Slough: NFER (revised edition but the standardization data is for the original edition of 1954)

WEBER, R. M. (1970) A linguistic analysis of first-grade reading errors *Reading Research Quarterly 5,* 427-51

Index of Names

Index of Subjects

Index of Names

Index of Subjects